DIRECTORY
OF
DEVOTIONAL PRAYER

Congregation
of Holy Cross

DIRECTORY
OF
DEVOTIONAL PRAYER

Congregation
of Holy Cross

Nihil Obstat   Rev. and Monsignor Michael Heintz, PhD
                  Censor Librorum
Imprimatur   Most Reverend Kevin C. Rhoades
                  Bishop of Fort Wayne–South Bend

Given at the Fort Wayne, Indiana, on 6 January 2012

The Nihil Obstat and Imprimatur are official declarations that a book or pamphlet is free of doctrinal or moral error. No implication is contained therein that those who have granted the Nihil Obstat or Imprimatur agree with its contents, opinions, or statements expressed.

Advisory Committee

Bro. Paul Bednarczyk, C.S.C., MPt
Rev. Joel Giallanza, C.S.C., MHP
Rev. Mario Lachapelle, C.S.C., C
Rev. Thomas Looney, C.S.C., DS
Rev. Peter Rocca, C.S.C. (US)
Rev. Kevin Russeau, C.S.C., O.S.
Rev. John Britto, C.S.C., VSC

Founded in 1865, Ave Maria Press is a ministry of the United States Province of Holy Cross.

www.avemariapress.com

ISBN-10 1-59471-300-6   ISBN-13 978-1-59471-300-2

Designed and produced by Ave Maria Press, Notre Dame, Ind.

Cover and text design by John R. Carson

Nihil Obstat: Reverend Monsignor Michael Heintz, PhD
                Censor Liborum
Imprimatur: Most Reverend Kevin C. Rhoades
                Bishop of Fort Wayne–South Bend
                Given at Fort Wayne, Indiana, on 6 January 2012

Scripture quotations are taken from the *Revised Standard Version* of the Bible, copyright © 1952 by the Division of Christian Education of the National Council of the Churches of Christ in the United States of America. Used by permission. All rights reserved.

Ad Hoc Committee
Bro. Paul Bednardczyk, C.S.C. (MP)
Bro. Joel Giallanza, C.S.C. (MP)
Rev. Mario Lachapelle, C.S.C. (C)
Rev. Thomas Looney, C.S.C. (US)
Rev. Peter Rocca, C.S.C. (US)
Rev. Kevin Russeau, C.S.C. (US)
Rev. John Vickers, C.S.C. (VEC)

Founded in 1865, Ave Maria Press is a ministry of the United States Province of Holy Cross.

www.avemariapress.com

ISBN-10 1-59471-300-6   ISBN-13 978-1-59471-300-2

Designed and produced by Ave Maria Press, Notre Dame, Indiana.

Cover and text design by John R. Carson.

Contents

Letter of Promulgation xv

Preface xvii

I. Holy Eucharist 1

Prayers before Mass 1

  1. Prayer (adapted from the 1859
     Directory) 1

  2. Prayer to the Eucharistic Heart of
     Jesus (1859 Directory) 3

  3. Act of Hope 5

  4. Act of Love 5

  5. Act of Desire 6

  6. Prayer to Saint Joseph 6

  7. Prayer of Saint Thomas Aquinas 7

  8. Prayer of Preparation for Holy
     Communion 8

  9. Prayer from the Byzantine Liturgy 9

Prayers after Mass 10

  10. Act of Thanksgiving (1859
     Directory) 10

  11. Act of Self-Offering (1859
     Directory) 12

  12. Act of Petition (1859 Directory) 13

13. *Anima Christi*—Prayer to the Most Holy Redeemer.............................. 13

14. Prayer to the Blessed Virgin Mary 14

15. Prayer of Saint Thomas Aquinas 15

16. Prayer of Saint Bonaventure 16

17. *Oblatio Sui*—Prayer of Self-Dedication to Jesus Christ (Saint Ignatius of Loyola)............................... 18

18. Prayer of Blessed John Newman......... 18

19. *En Ego*—Prayer to Jesus Christ Crucified.. 19

Visit to the Blessed Sacrament........................ 20

20. Act of Faith (1859 Directory) 20

21. Act of Hope (1859 Directory) 21

22. Act of Love (1859 Directory) 22

23. Act of Desire (1859 Directory) 23

24. Prayer of Blessed John Newman......... 24

25. Prayer of Adoration............................. 24

26. Prayer to Jesus in the Holy Eucharist.. 25

27. Four Short Prayers to the Eucharistic Heart of Jesus 26

28. *Adoro Te Devote* (Saint Thomas Aquinas) 28

29. *Pange Lingua* (Saint Thomas Aquinas) 29

30. Litany of the Holy Eucharist 30

Benediction of the Most Blessed Sacrament... 33
   31. Rite of Eucharistic Exposition and
      Benediction 33

II. Daily Meditation.. 39
   32. Prayer before Meditation..................... 40
   33. At the Beginning of Meditation.......... 40
   34. Prayers before Reading Scripture........ 41
   35. To Mary Immaculate 42
   36. Prayer after Meditation 42
   37. O Jesus, Living in Mary
      (Jean-Jacques Olier, S.S.) 43
   38. *Suscipe* (Saint Ignatius of Loyola) 43
   39. Serenity Prayer (Reinhold Niebuhr) ... 44

III. Particular Examen 47
   40. Order of Examen 48

IV. Sacrament of Reconciliation 55
   41. Prayer before Examination of
      Conscience 56
   42. Examination of Conscience (based on
      the Constitutions of the Congregation
      of Holy Cross) 57
   43. Prayer before Confession.................... 68
   44. Prayer for Contrition.......................... 69
   45. Act of Contrition 69

V. Stations of the Cross................................ 71
    46. Stations of the Cross (I) 72
    47. Stations of the Cross (II).................... 94
VI. Prayers 115
   Prayers for Holy Cross 116
    48. Weekly Prayers for Vocations to the
        Congregation of Holy Cross 116
    49. For Vocations................................... 120
    50. For the Congregation of
        Holy Cross....................................... 121
    51. For the Family of Holy Cross (I)...... 122
    52. For the Family of Holy Cross (II) 123
    53. For the Family of Holy Cross (III) ... 124
    54. For Holy Cross Collaborators and
        Associates.. 125
    55. For Those to Whom We Minister 126
    56. For Perseverance in Religious Life 127
    57. For Personal Renewal of Vows.......... 128
    58. For a Spirit of Obedience (from the
        Spiritual Exercises for the Marianites
        of Holy Cross by Father Moreau)....... 129
    59. For Those in Authority in the
        Congregation................................... 129
    60. For Our Benefactors 130
   Prayers for a Dying Religious 131
    61. Litany for a Dying Religious
        (adapted from the 1947 Directory
        and Pastoral Care of the Sick, 1983) .. 132

62. Prayer by a Dying Religious
    (adapted from the 1947 Directory) 135
63. Prayer of Commendation 137
64. Prayer after Death (I) 138
65. Prayer after Death (II) 139
Intercessory Prayers and Prayers for
Individual Canonizations 140
66. For the Intercession of Blessed Basil
    Moreau and Saint André Bessette 140
67. For the Canonization of Our
    Servants of God 143
68. Additional Prayers for Individual
    Canonizations 144
    • Blessed Basil Moreau 144
    • Blessed Marie-Léonie Paradis 144
    • Servant of God Patrick Peyton 145
    • Servant of God Theotonius Amal
      Ganguly 146
    • Servant of God Vincent Joseph
      McCauley 146
    • Servant of God Flavien Laplante 147
    • Jacques-François Dujarié (1947
      Directory) 148
69. For a Favor through the
    Intercession of: 149
    • Blessed Marie-Léonie Paradis 149

- Servants of God Patrick Peyton, Theotonius Ganguly, or Vincent McCauley 149
- Servant of God Flavien Laplante 150
- Jacques-François Dujarié 151

Other Prayers.. 152
70. For the Pope (I)............................... 152
71. For the Pope (II) (from the Roman Missal) 153
72. For the Local Church (from the Roman Missal)................................. 154
73. For the Diocesan Bishop (from the Roman Missal) 154
74. For Government and World Leaders (based on 1988 Constitutions)............ 155
75. *Veni, Creator Spiritus* 156
76. For the Invocation of the Seven Gifts of the Holy Spirit (Saint Bonaventure).. 158
77. To the Holy Spirit............................ 160
78. For Spiritual Discernment (Saint Benedict)....................................... 161
79. For Justice and Peace (based on 1988 Constitutions)............................ 162
80. For the Poor and the Oppressed....... 163
81. For Giving Thanks to God for the Gift of Human Life (from the Roman Missal)................................. 164

82. For the Sick 164

83. For Families 165

84. Litany of Saints 167

VII. Principal Patrons............................... 171

Saint Joseph... 172

85. *Memorare* in Honor of
Saint Joseph 173

86. Consecration to Saint Joseph............ 173

87. Prayer to Saint Joseph (especially
after the recitation of the Rosary) 174

88. To Obtain a Special Favor 176

89. For Vocations to Holy Cross 177

90. Prayer to Saint Joseph, Patron of
Holy Cross (adapted from the 1947
Directory).. 178

91. Prayers to Saint Joseph (from the
Votive Chapel of Saint Joseph's
Oratory, Montréal, Canada) 179

• Joseph, Our Solace in Suffering....... 179

• Joseph, Model of Laborers.............. 180

• Joseph, Mainstay of Families 181

• Joseph, Hope of the Sick................. 181

• Joseph, Patron of the Dying............ 182

• Joseph, Protector of the Church 183

• Joseph, Terror of Demons............... 184

• Joseph, Guardian of the Pure
of Heart.. 185

92. The Joys and Sorrows of Saint Joseph 185

93. Prayer to Saint Joseph for a Happy Death (I) 196

94. Prayer to Saint Joseph for a Happy Death (II) 197

95. Litany of Saint Joseph 198

The Blessed Virgin Mary, Our Lady of Sorrows 200

96. *Memorare* 200

97. *Sub Tuum Præsidium* 201

98. An Ancient Prayer to Our Lady 201

99. *Tota Pulchra Es* 202

100. Consecration to the Blessed Virgin Mary (1859 Directory) 202

101. Vocation Prayer to Mary, Mother of Sorrows 203

102. The Chaplet of Our Lady of Sorrows 205

103. The Rosary of the Blessed Virgin Mary 208

104. *Angelus* 217

105. Marian Anthems 218

 • *Alma Redemptoris Mater* 218

 • *Ave Regina Cælorum* 219

 • *Regina Cæli* 220

 • *Salve Regina* 221

106. Litany of the Blessed Virgin Mary
(Litany of Loreto) 222

The Sacred Heart of Jesus 225

107. *Memorare* to the Sacred Heart 225

108. Prayer to the Sacred Heart
of Jesus 226

109. Act of Consecration to the Sacred
Heart (Saint Margaret Mary
Alacoque) 227

110. Consecration to the Sacred Heart
(1947 Directory) 228

111. Prayers to the Sacred Heart (1859
Directory) 229

112. Invocations to the Sacred Heart 231

113. Litany of the Sacred Heart
of Jesus 232

Via Framura, 85
00168 Rome—Italy

Phone (39) 06-612-962-10
Fax (39) 06-614-7547

Congregation of Holy Cross
General Administration

Richard V. Warner, C.S.C.
Superior General

September 15, 2011

For the past several years, the Reverend Peter D. Rocca, C.S.C., has chaired an ad hoc committee to prepare a directory of prayer for the use of the members of the Congregation of Holy Cross at the request of the Reverend Hugh W. Cleary, C.S.C., who at that time served as Superior General. In 2009, the members of the Council of the Congregation approved the concept of a directory of prayer, which the committee developed. Subsequently, Father Cleary and his Council approved the directory of prayer that had been developed and placed its promulgation on the agenda of the 2010 General Chapter.

At the 2010 General Chapter, the delegates welcomed this book and unanimously recommended its promulgation and distribution, in the following words: "The

Chapter commends the work done in preparing *The Directory of Devotional Prayer*. The Chapter recommends its promulgation and distribution." (See Recommendation 15, *Proceedings of the General Chapter*.)

With the consent of the members of the General Council, I hereby promulgate the publication of *The Directory of Devotional Prayer.*

I am confident that the *Directory* will serve the needs of many members of the Congregation. I thank the ad hoc committee for bringing this important project to such a successful conclusion.

Given in Rome on this 15th day of September in the Year of Our Lord 2011, on the occasion of the Solemnity of Our Lady of Sorrows, and on the 154th anniversary of the Papal Approbation of the Rules of the Institute of the Congregation of Holy Cross.

Richard V. Warner, csc

Richard V. Warner, C.S.C.
Superior General

Preface

AS THE liturgical prayer of the Church expresses and forms us in the faith of the Church, so this *Directory of Devotional Prayer* expresses and forms us in the spiritual heritage of the Congregation of Holy Cross. The prayers and texts chosen for inclusion in this book of prayers were taken from the writings of Father Moreau, the Church's rich patrimony of popular devotions, or were newly composed in light of our Constitutions, charism, and spiritual heritage.

Although Blessed Basil Moreau taught that the "gospel is quite sufficient as a rule of life for religious," he provided his first religious with Constitutions and Rules, as well as a Directory, a book of common and personal prayers, to assist in their ongoing formation and living of the religious life. By the publication of this *Directory of Devotional Prayer*, the Congregation invites us to enhance our personal prayer, already marked by meditation upon the Scriptures and our Constitutions, with a prayerful engagement of the "sound popular devotions" proposed in this text. Thus, the traditional triptych of Scripture, Constitutions and Rules, and a book of prayer, offered by Father Moreau as the principal texts for our common formation and transformation in prayer, is restored.

This *Directory of Devotional Prayer* forms us in the spiritual heritage of Holy Cross in four principal ways. First, it proposes the principal elements of our Holy Cross tradition (Eucharistic devotion, daily meditation, examination of conscience and preparation for Reconciliation, the Way of the Cross, vocal prayers for various needs, and devotion to Saint Joseph, Our Lady of Sorrows, and the Sacred Heart of Jesus) for our personal prayer and reflection. In so doing, it deepens our bonds with the "great band of men" who beckoned us to "walk in their company" and who ground us in our historical patrimony.

Second, it enhances these traditional elements by providing a context and texts from the Scripture and our Constitutions. Thus, it complements our historical patrimony with the Word of God, which speaks to us anew in every age, and our Constitutions, which summon us to ever greater fidelity to Christ in the present moment.

Third, this *Directory of Devotional Prayer* invites us to contemplate the lives of our holy predecessors in Holy Cross. Thus, it calls to mind that our life in Holy Cross is a genuine way of holiness and that in our journey of faith we are not alone as we come before the Lord in prayer.

Fourth, it proposes for prayer and meditation the dynamic elements of the Holy Cross charism: conformity to Christ, trust in Divine Providence, confidence in the Cross, and a spirit of union and collaboration. In so doing, it reminds us that our way of life in Holy Cross, a path of holiness, is meant, as Moreau dreamed it, to be "a powerful lever with which to move, direct and sanctify the whole world."

Our Constitutions speak of God's Spirit, who "gives us the desire and utterance for prayer," and of prayer as "our faith attending to the Lord." May this *Directory of Devotional Prayer*, a testament of faith attending to the Lord, help to stir to flame within our hearts the desire for God that is always the Spirit's gift!

Holy Eucharist

There can be no Christian community which does not gather in worship and in prayer. It is true of the church and true as well of Holy Cross. The Lord's supper is the church's foremost gathering for prayer. It is our duty and need to break that bread and share that cup every day unless prevented by serious cause. We are fortified for the journey on which he has sent us. We find ourselves especially close as a brotherhood when we share this greatest of all table fellowships. (*Constitution 3:27*)

Prayers before Mass

1. Prayer
(adapted from the 1859 Directory)

O my God, I adore and acknowledge you as my
    Lord.
Everything that I am and possess comes from you.
Since you deserve unconditional honor and praise
and I am unable to return the fullness of your love,
I offer you and unite myself to the unconditional
love and obedience of Jesus your Son,
who offers himself to you in the mystery of this
    Eucharist.

As Jesus does, I wish to do;
in union with him I offer myself to you.
In union with him I surrender myself to your will.
In union with him I adore you and give my heart
    to you.

As Jesus prays, I wish to pray;
In union with him I pray for the forgiveness of my
    enemies.
In union with him I pray for the consolation of
    your Spirit.
In union with him I pray that you will receive my
    spirit.

O my God, deepen my love for Jesus your Son
through my participation in this Eucharist

so that my thoughts, conduct, actions, and
    affections
may be more deeply conformed to his.
Amen.

---

2. PRAYER TO THE EUCHARISTIC HEART OF JESUS
(1859 Directory)

Eucharistic Heart, sovereign love of the Lord Jesus,
who instituted this venerable sacrament
in order to remain in our midst and to give us
your Body and Blood as heavenly food and drink;
I firmly believe, Lord Jesus, in your supreme love
which instituted the Holy Eucharist;
and here before this Most Blessed Sacrament,
it is most appropriate that I adore this love of
    yours,
that I praise and exalt it as the great source of life
    in your church.
Your love is for me a pressing invitation;
for you seem to be saying to me: "See how much
    I have loved you!
In giving you my flesh to eat and my blood to drink,
I desire by this union to awaken your charity
and to unite you to myself.

I desire to transform your soul into me, the bread
    of eternal life.
So give me your heart, live in my life, and you
    shall live in God."
I acknowledge, Lord, the longing of your
    Eucharistic Heart,
and for it I give you my sincere thanks.
My heart is ready, yes, my heart is ready to
    accept your invitation.
Give me the grace of being penetrated
through and through by this divine love, where
    you invite me,
like the disciples before your sacred passion,
to take and eat your holy Body and Blood.

Engrave deeply within my heart the firm purpose
of being ever faithful to your loving invitation.
Grant me the devotion and reverence needed
to honor and receive worthily the precious gift
of your Eucharistic Heart, the gift of your
    dying love.
With the help of your grace,
enable me to celebrate fruitfully the memorial
    of your passion,
to make due reparation for my offences
    and ambivalence,

to nourish and increase my love for you,
and to preserve ever-living within my heart
the seeds of a blessed eternity.

3. ACT OF HOPE

Good Jesus, in you alone I place all my hope.
You are my salvation and my strength, the source
    of all good.
Through your mercy, through your passion
    and death,
I hope to obtain pardon of my sins,
the grace of final perseverance,
and a happy eternity.
Amen.

4. ACT OF LOVE

Jesus, my God, I love you with my whole heart
    and above all things
because you are the one supreme good and an
    infinitely perfect being.
You have given your life for me, a poor sinner,
and in your mercy you have even offered yourself as
    food for my soul.

My God, I love you.
Inflame my heart to love you more.
Amen.

---

5. ACT OF DESIRE

Jesus, my God and my all, my soul longs for you.
My heart yearns to receive you in Holy Communion.
Come, bread of heaven and food of angels, to
    nourish my soul and to rejoice my heart.
Come, most lovable friend of my soul, to inflame
    me with such love
that I may never again be separated from you.
Amen.

---

6. PRAYER TO SAINT JOSEPH

Happy and blessed are you, O Joseph, to whom it
    has been given
not only to see and hear but also to bear in your
    arms, to embrace, to clothe,
and to watch over God himself,
whom many kings have desired to see but have not
    seen,
and to hear but have not heard.

Pray for us, O blessed Joseph.
 —*That we may be worthy of the promises of Christ.*

✣ ✣ ✣ ✣ ✣ ✣ ✣

I am nothing . . . only a tool in the hands of
Providence, a lowly instrument at the service
of Saint Joseph.

—**Saint André Bessette**

✣ ✣ ✣ ✣ ✣ ✣ ✣ ✣ ✣

7. PRAYER OF SAINT THOMAS AQUINAS

Almighty and eternal God, I approach the sacrament of your only-begotten Son, our Lord Jesus Christ. As a sick person I approach the physician of life; as one unclean, I come to the fountain of mercy; blind, to the light of eternal brightness; poor and needy, to the Lord of heaven and earth. I beseech you, therefore, in your boundless mercy, to heal my sickness, to wash away my defilements, to enlighten my blindness, to enrich my poverty, and to clothe my nakedness.

Let me receive the bread of angels, the King of kings, the Lord of lords, with such reverence and humility, such contrition and faith, such purpose and intention, as may help the salvation of my soul. Grant, I beseech you, that I may receive not only the Sacrament of the Body and Blood of our Lord but also the whole grace and virtue of the Sacrament.

O most indulgent God, grant me so to receive the Body of your only-begotten Son, our Lord Jesus Christ, which he took of the Virgin Mary, that I may be found worthy to be incorporated with his mystical body and numbered among his members.

O most loving Father, grant that I may one day forever contemplate him unveiled and face-to-face, whom, on my pilgrimage, I receive under a veil, your beloved Son, who lives and reigns with you and the Holy Spirit, one God, forever and ever. Amen.

8. PRAYER OF PREPARATION FOR HOLY COMMUNION

O Lord Jesus Christ, King of everlasting glory,
　　behold, I desire to come to you
and to receive your Body and Blood in this
　　heavenly sacrament,
for your honor and glory, and the good of my soul.

I desire to receive you because it is your desire and
   you have so willed it.
Blessed be your name forever! I desire to come to
   you like Magdalene,
that I may be delivered from all my evils, and
   embrace you, my only good.
I desire to come to you that I may be happily
   united to you,
that I will henceforth abide in you, and you in me,
and that nothing in life or death may ever separate
   me from you.
Amen.

---

9. Prayer from the Byzantine Liturgy

O Lord, I believe and profess that you are truly
   Christ, the Son of the living God,
who came into the world to save sinners, of whom
   I am the first.
Accept me as a partaker of your mystical supper, O
   Son of God, for I will not reveal your mystery to
   your enemies, but like the thief I confess to you:
Remember me, O Lord, when you shall come into
   your kingdom.
Remember me, O Master, when you shall come
   into your kingdom.

Remember me, O Holy One, when you shall come
    into your kingdom.

May the partaking of your holy mysteries, O Lord,
    be not for my judgment or condemnation, but
    for the healing of soul and body.

O Lord, I also believe and profess that this, which I
    am about to receive, is truly your most precious
    Body and your life-giving Blood which, I pray,
    make me worthy to receive for the remission of
    my sins and for life everlasting.

Amen.

✛ ✛ ✛ ✛ ✛ ✛ ✛

Prayers after Mass

10. ACT OF THANKSGIVING
(1859 Directory)

What thanksgiving, O my God,
will equal the favor you have bestowed upon me?
Not content with having loved me as far as to die
    for my sake, God of goodness,

you chose also to come personally and honor me
    with your presence,
giving yourself to me. O my soul, glorify the Lord
    your God,
confess his goodness, exalt his magnificence, show
    forth eternally God's mercy.
It is with a heart melting and filled with gratitude,
    O my sweet Savior,
that I return thanks to you for the graces you have
    chosen to grant me.
I have been unfaithful, cowardly, and quibbling,
    but I will not be ungrateful.
I will eternally remember that this day you have
    given yourself to me,
and throughout the remainder of my life I will give
    myself entirely to you.
Amen.

✠ ✠ ✠ ✠ ✠ ✠ ✠

*Let us not forget that the development of the work
entrusted to us depends upon our acceptance of the
inspirations of grace and our fidelity in seconding the
designs of Divine Providence.*
    —Blessed Basil Moreau (*Circular Letter 23*)

✠ ✠ ✠ ✠ ✠ ✠ ✠

11. ACT OF SELF-OFFERING
(1859 Directory)

My beloved is mine and I am his.
Yes, O my God, all is consummated;
you have given yourself entirely to me,
and I give myself entirely to you.
I come to offer myself undivided and irretrievably;
in short, I will be yours forever.
I offer you my understanding
that it may be engaged in contemplating your
     greatness.
I offer you my memory that it may call to mind
     your blessings.
I offer you my heart that it may dedicate to you
all its sentiments, its affections, and its inclinations.
I offer you my body and senses to devote them to
     your service and good pleasure.
I offer you and I dedicate to you, my Savior, all
     that I have and all that I am.
All is yours!
Amen.

12. ACT OF PETITION
(1859 Directory)

O my adorable Savior,

since you have come into me to grant me your
grace, and you wish that I should demand it,

I desire neither the good things of the earth,
nor riches, nor honors, nor the joys of this
world.

I entreat you to grant me a great and deep sorrow
for the sins I have committed against you.

Grant me fidelity to your grace, holy fervor in
your service, and your holy love and final
perseverance in your service.

Amen.

13. *ANIMA CHRISTI*
Prayer to the Most Holy Redeemer

Soul of Christ, sanctify me.
Body of Christ, save me.
Blood of Christ, inebriate me.
Water from the side of Christ, wash me.
Passion of Christ, strengthen me.
O good Jesus, hear me.

Within your wounds, hide me.
Separated from you let me never be.
From the malignant enemy, defend me,
That I may praise you in the company of your
    saints for all eternity.
Amen.

14. PRAYER TO THE BLESSED VIRGIN MARY

Mary, holy Virgin Mother,
I have received your Son, Jesus Christ.
With love you became his mother, gave birth
    to him, nursed him, and helped him grow to
    manhood.
With love I return him to you, to hold once more,
    to love with all your heart,
and to offer to the Holy Trinity as our supreme act
    of worship for your honor and the good
    of all your pilgrim brothers and sisters.
Mother, ask God to forgive my sins
and to help me to serve him more faithfully.
Keep me true to Christ until death,
and let me come to praise him with you
forever and ever.
Amen.

15. Prayer of Saint Thomas Aquinas

Lord, Father, all-powerful and ever-living God,
I thank you, for even though I am a sinner, your
    unprofitable servant,
not because of my worth but in the kindness of
    your mercy,
you fed me with the precious Body and Blood of
    your Son, our Lord Jesus Christ.
I pray that this Holy Communion may not bring
    me condemnation and punishment
but forgiveness and salvation.
May it be a helmet of faith and a shield of goodwill.
May it purify me from evil ways and put an end to
    my evil passions.
May it bring me charity and patience, humility and
    obedience, and growth in the power to do good.
May it be my strong defense against all enemies,
    visible and invisible,
and the perfect calming of all my evil impulses,
    bodily and spiritual.
May it unite me more closely to you, the one true
    God,
and lead me safely through death to everlasting
    happiness with you.
And I pray that you will lead me, a sinner, to the

banquet where you, with your Son and Holy Spirit,
are true and perfect light, total fulfillment,
everlasting joy, gladness without end,
and perfect happiness to your saints.
Grant this through Christ our Lord.
Amen.

✝ ✝✝ ✝ ✝ ✝ ✝ ✝ ✝ ✝

When praying, one speaks to God like a friend.

—Saint André Bessette

✝ ✝ ✝ ✝ ✝ ✝ ✝

16. PRAYER OF SAINT BONAVENTURE

Pierce, O most sweet Jesus, my inmost soul
with the most joyous and healthful wound of your
love,
with true, serene, and most apostolic charity,
that my soul may ever languish and melt with love
and longing for you,
that it may yearn for you and faint for your courts,
and long to be dissolved and to be with you.
Grant that my soul may hunger after you, the bread
of angels,

the refreshment of holy souls, our daily and super-
    substantial bread,
having all sweetness and savor and every delight of
    taste;
let my heart ever hunger after and feed upon you,
upon whom the angels desire to look,
and may my inmost soul be filled with the
    sweetness of your savor;
may it thirst after you, the fountain of eternal light,
the torrent of pleasure, the richness of the house of
    God;
may it ever compass you, seek you, find you, run to
    you,
attain you, meditate upon you, speak of you, with
    humility and discretion,
with love and delight, with ease and affection,
and with perseverance unto the end;
may you alone be ever my hope, my entire
    assurance,
my riches, my delight, my pleasure, my joy, my rest
    and tranquility,
my peace, my sweetness, my fragrance, my sweet
    savor, my food,
my refreshment, my refuge, my help, my wisdom,
    my portion,
my possession, and my treasure,
in whom may my mind and my heart be fixed

and firm and rooted immovably henceforth and
     forever.
Amen.

---

17. OBLATIO SUI

Prayer of Self-Dedication to Jesus Christ
(Saint Ignatius of Loyola)

Lord Jesus Christ,
take all my freedom, my memory, my
     understanding, and my will.
All that I have and cherish you have given me.
I surrender it all to be guided by your will.
Your grace and your love are wealth enough for
     me.
Give me these, Lord Jesus, and I ask for nothing
     more.

---

18. PRAYER OF BLESSED JOHN NEWMAN

Dear Jesus,
help me to spread your fragrance everywhere I go.
Flood my soul with your spirit and life.
Penetrate and possess my whole being so utterly
that my life may only be a radiance of yours.

Shine through me and be so in me that every soul I
    come in contact with
may feel your presence in my soul.
Let them look up and see no longer me, but only
    you, Jesus!
Stay with me, and then I shall begin to shine as you
    shine,
so to shine as to be a light to others.
The light, O Jesus, will be all from you; none of it
    will be mine.
It will be you, shining on others through me.
Let me thus praise you in the way you love best,
by shining on those around me.
Let me preach you without preaching,
not by words but by example,
by the catching force, the sympathetic influence of
    what I do, the evident fullness of the love
    my heart bears for you.
Amen.

---

19. EN EGO
Prayer to Jesus Christ Crucified

My good and dear Jesus,
I kneel before you, asking you most earnestly
to engrave upon my heart

a deep and lively faith, hope, and charity,
with true repentance for my sins,
and a firm resolve to make amends.
As I reflect upon your five wounds,
and dwell upon them with deep compassion and
    grief,
I recall, good Jesus, the words the prophet David
    spoke long ago concerning yourself:
"They have pierced my hands and my feet;
they have counted all my bones!"

✢ ✢ ✢ ✢ ✢ ✢ ✢ ✢

Visit to the
Blessed Sacrament

20. ACT OF FAITH
(1859 Directory)

I believe, O my Savior,
that you are really and substantially present
under these appearances which offer themselves to
    my sight.

I am sure that they are no more bread and wine;
they are your adorable Body and your precious
  Blood,
for you have proclaimed it so, O Lord,
you who are truth itself,
and I know that all things obey your sacred and all-
  powerful voice.
Amen.

---

21. ACT OF HOPE
(1859 Directory)

My God, my Lord,
I hope in you, and I shall not be confounded.
I will see you one day. I will possess you in heaven.
You will fill me with joy by the sight of your face,
and you will show me all that is good in knowing
  you, and I shall live forever.
This is my hope, this is my life.
Amen.

22. ACT OF LOVE
(1859 Directory)

Come, Lord Jesus,
come, O desired of nations, light of the world,
delight of the Eternal Father, and object of the
    Father's love.
You desire that in approaching these mysteries
I remember you, my God.
I will never forget your benefits, or the infinite love
which has led you to bestow on me so many
    blessings.
O my Savior,
I will remember that being one with the Father
your desire to come to us led you to take human
    flesh.
I will remember that having taken this flesh for my
    sake
that you also sacrificed it for my salvation.
And now, O my Savior,
not satisfied with having taken flesh for my
    salvation in the Incarnation,
and having given it for my sake on the Cross,
you give it to me in this adorable sacrament.
Amen.

✠ ✠ ✠ ✠ ✠ ✠ ✠

*Prayer consists less of words than of desires and
aspirations of the heart that need no long formulas nor
abundance of word. Prayer is a fervent and continuous
desire.*

—Blessed Basil Moreau (*Exercises of 1858*)

✠ ✠ ✠ ✠ ✠ ✠ ✠

23. ACT OF DESIRE
(1859 Directory)

Come, O adorable Savior,
come into a soul that longs for you
as a thirsty deer for a spring.
Draw me to yourself; turn me into you, be in me,
    and let me be in you,
as your Father is in you and you are in the Father.
Come and live in me that I may no more be mine,
and that I may be intimately united to you so as to
    be one with you.
I cannot live any longer without you.
Come and enliven my soul;
may I be entirely consumed by your love.
Amen.

24. PRAYER OF BLESSED JOHN NEWMAN

I place myself in the presence of him,
in whose incarnate presence I am before I place
    myself there.
I adore you, O my Savior, present here as God and
    as man,
in soul and in body, in true flesh and blood.
I acknowledge and confess that I kneel before that
    sacred humanity,
which was conceived in Mary's womb, and lay in
    Mary's bosom;
which grew up to twelve, wrought miracles,
and spoke words of wisdom and peace;
which in due season hung on the Cross, lay in the
    tomb,
rose from the dead, and now reigns in heaven.
I praise, and bless, and give myself wholly to him,
who is the true Bread of my soul, and my
    everlasting joy.

25. PRAYER OF ADORATION

I adore you, Jesus, true God and true man,
present in the Holy Eucharist,
kneeling before you and united in spirit

with all the faithful on earth and all the saints in
   heaven.
In gratitude for so great a blessing, I love you with
   all my heart,
for you are worthy of all praise and adoration.
Lord Jesus Christ,
may I never offend you with my lack of love.
May your Eucharistic presence refresh me in body
   and soul.
Mary, Mother of the Eucharistic Lord, pray for me
and obtain for me a greater love for Jesus.
Amen.

26. PRAYER TO JESUS IN THE HOLY EUCHARIST

My Lord Jesus Christ,
your Eucharistic presence teaches me
how to love you as you loved me.
In your great love for me
you continue to give yourself, body, blood, soul,
   and divinity,
in this sacrament of your love.
As I pray here in your Eucharistic presence,
enkindle in me the fire of your Gospel.
Nourish me with your love and compassion,

so that I may be your living presence to all I meet.
Amen.

27. FOUR SHORT PRAYERS TO THE EUCHARISTIC HEART OF JESUS

I

Eucharistic Heart of Jesus,
fill my heart with that same love
that burned in your heart.
May I become love and mercy
to those who live in pain and suffering.
May I become the living Gospel
of your compassionate love.

II

Eucharistic Heart of Jesus,
fill me with faith, hope, and love.
When I find myself lacking in charity,
help me to see your presence
in those around me.
Increase my faith
when I find it hard to understand.
Give me hope when life around me
seems empty and forsaken.
May your presence

in the Blessed Sacrament of the altar
be my courage and strength.

III

Eucharistic Heart of Jesus,
your gift of the Holy Eucharist
strengthens me on the journey of life.
Transform me into your disciple and send me
to those who are in need of your love.
May I be your hands to those who are helpless.
May I be your heart to those who are unloved.
Summon me with your light and allow me
to be an instrument of your peace and joy.

IV

Eucharistic Heart of Jesus,
many times I find life to be difficult
and filled with anxiety.
Help me in times of uncertainty
to come into your Eucharistic presence.
Be my strength, my rock, my fortress, and my
    refuge.
Help me, by the power of your Holy Spirit,
to feel the light of your resurrection,
surrounding me and protecting me from all danger.
In you I hope, Lord;
may I never be disappointed.

28. ADORO TE DEVOTE
(Saint Thomas Aquinas)

I adore you devoutly, Godhead unseen,
who truly lies hidden under these sacramental
    forms.
My soul surrenders itself to you without reserve,
for in contemplating you it is completely
    overwhelmed.
Sight, touch, and taste are no guide in finding you,
and only hearing is a sure guide for our faith.
I believe everything that the Son of God has said,
and nothing can be truer than this word of the
    Truth.
Only the Godhead was hidden on the Cross,
but here the humanity is hidden as well.
Yet, I believe and acknowledge them both
and make the same request as did the repentant
    thief.
I do not see the marks of the wounds, as Thomas
    did,
and yet I, too, own you as "My God."
Grant that I believe in you more and more,
that I put my hope in you, and that I love you.
Living Bread, that ever recalls the Lord's death
and gives life to his servants,

grant to my soul to live by you
and always to taste your sweetness.
Lord Jesus, loving Pelican of heaven,
cleanse me, a sinner, with your Blood,
for a single drop can save the whole world from all
    its sin.
Jesus, as I look on your veiled presence,
I pray that what I long for so ardently may come
    about,
and that I may see your face unveiled
and be happy in the vision of your glory.
Amen.

29. PANGE LINGUA
(Saint Thomas Aquinas)

Praise, my tongue, the mystery of the glorious
    Body and of the precious Blood
which the king of nations, fruit of a royal womb,
    poured out as the world's ransom.
To us he was given, to us he was born of a pure
    Virgin.
He lived in the world, and when he had spread the
    seed of truth,
he closed in a wondrous way the period of his
    sojourn here.

As he is reclining with his brethren on the night of
the Last Supper,
he complies completely with the Law in regard to
the legal foods
and then gives himself with his own hands as food
to the group of twelve.
The Word made flesh by a word changes true bread
into his flesh, and wine becomes his blood.
If one cannot perceive this change,
faith of itself is enough to convince the well
disposed.
Let us, therefore, humbly reverence so great a
sacrament.
Let the old types depart and give way to the new
rite.
Let faith provide her help where all the senses fail.
To the Father and the Son be praise, acclamation,
salvation, honor, might, and blessing, too.
To the One who proceeds from them both be
given equal praise.
Amen.

30. LITANY OF THE HOLY EUCHARIST

Lord, have mercy   Lord, have mercy
Christ, have mercy   Christ, have mercy
Lord, have mercy   Lord have mercy

Jesus, the Most High	have mercy on us
Jesus, the Holy One	have mercy on us
Jesus, Word of God	have mercy on us
Jesus, only Son of the Father	have mercy on us
Jesus, Son of Mary	have mercy on us
Jesus, crucified for us	have mercy on us
Jesus, risen from the dead	have mercy on us
Jesus, reigning in glory	have mercy on us
Jesus, coming in glory	have mercy on us
Jesus, our Lord	have mercy on us
Jesus, our hope	have mercy on us
Jesus, our peace	have mercy on us
Jesus, our Savior	have mercy on us
Jesus, our salvation	have mercy on us
Jesus, our resurrection	have mercy on us
Jesus, Judge of all	have mercy on us
Jesus, Lord of the Church	have mercy on us
Jesus, Lord of creation	have mercy on us
Jesus, Lover of all	have mercy on us
Jesus, life of the world	have mercy on us
Jesus, freedom for the imprisoned	have mercy on us
Jesus, joy of the sorrowing	have mercy on us
Jesus, giver of the Spirit	have mercy on us
Jesus, giver of good gifts	have mercy on us
Jesus, source of new life	have mercy on us
Jesus, Lord of life	have mercy on us
Jesus, eternal high priest	have mercy on us
Jesus, priest and victim	have mercy on us

Jesus, true Shepherd	have mercy on us
Jesus, true light	have mercy on us
Jesus, bread of heaven	have mercy on us
Jesus, bread of life	have mercy on us
Jesus, bread of thanksgiving	have mercy on us
Jesus, life-giving bread	have mercy on us
Jesus, holy manna	have mercy on us
Jesus, food for everlasting life	have mercy on us
Jesus, food for our journey	have mercy on us
Jesus, holy banquet	have mercy on us
Jesus, true Sacrifice	have mercy on us
Jesus, divine Victim	have mercy on us
Jesus, Mediator of the new covenant	have mercy on us
Jesus, mystery of the altar	have mercy on us
Jesus, mystery of faith	have mercy on us
Jesus, medicine of immortality	have mercy on us
Jesus, pledge of eternal glory	have mercy on us
Jesus, Lamb of God, you take away the sins of the world	have mercy on us
Jesus, Bearer of our sins, you take away the sins of the world	have mercy on us
Jesus, Redeemer of the world, you take away the sins of the world	have mercy on us
Christ, hear us	Christ, hear us
Christ, graciously hear us	Christ, graciously hear us
Lord Jesus, hear our prayer	Lord Jesus, hear our prayer

✠ ✠ ✠ ✠ ✠ ✠ ✠ ✠ ✠

Benediction of the Most Blessed Sacrament

31. RITE OF EUCHARISTIC EXPOSITION AND BENEDICTION

Exposition

After the minister exposes the Blessed Sacrament according to the ritual, "O Salutaris" or some other appropriate hymn is sung.

O Salutaris Hostia

O salutaris Hostia
Quæ cæli pandis ostium.
Bella premunt hostilia;
Da robur fer auxilium.

Uni trinoque Domino
Sit sempiterna gloria:

Qui vitam sine termino,
Nobis donet in patria.
Amen.

O Saving Victim opening wide
The gate of heav'n to us below.
Our foes press on from every side;
Thine aid supply, Thy strength bestow.

To Thy great name be endless praise,
Immortal Godhead, One in Three;
Oh, grant us endless length of days,
In our true native land with Thee.
Amen.

Adoration

It is recommended that there be an extended period for
adoration, which may include both silent and communal
prayer, hymns, and readings to direct the attention of the
faithful to the worship of Christ the Lord. (See "Visit to the
Blessed Sacrament," nos. 20–30, for suggested prayers.)

Benediction

Toward the end of the Eucharistic Adoration, the minister,
kneeling, incenses the Blessed Sacrament while "Tantum
Ergo," or some other appropriate hymn, is sung.

Tantum Ergo

Tantum ergo Sacramentum
Veneremur cernui;
Et antiquum documentum
Novo cedat ritui;
Præstet fides supplementum
Sensuum defectui.

Genitori, Genitoque,
Laus et iubilatio;
Salus, honor, virtus quoque
Sit et benedictio:
Procedenti ab utroque
Compar sit laudatio.
Amen.

Down in adoration falling
Lo! The Sacred Host we hail.
Lo! O'er ancient forms departing,
Newer rites of grace prevail;
Faith for all defects supplying
Where the feeble senses fail.

To the Everlasting Father,
And the Son who reigns on high,
With the Holy Ghost proceeding
Forth from each eternally,

Be salvation, honor, blessing,
Might, and endless majesty.
Amen.

*The minister then sings (or says) the versicle, and the people
respond.*

You have given them bread from heaven. (Alleluia.)
   —*Having all sweetness within it. (Alleluia.)*

The minister stands and continues:

Let us pray.

Lord Jesus Christ,
you gave us the Eucharist
as the memorial of your suffering and death.
May our worship of this Sacrament of your Body
     and Blood
help us to experience the salvation you won for us
and the peace of the Kingdom,
where you live with the Father and the Holy Spirit,
one God, forever and ever.
Amen.

*After the prayer, a priest or deacon puts on the humeral
veil, genuflects, and, taking the monstrance, makes the Sign*

of the Cross over the people in silence. Otherwise, the blessing is omitted.

Reposition

As the Blessed Sacrament is reposed in the tabernacle, the following, or some other acclamation or hymn, may be used.

Holy God, we praise Thy name!
Lord of all, we bow before Thee;
All on earth Thy scepter claim,
All in heav'n above adore Thee;
Infinite Thy vast domain,
Everlasting is Thy reign.

Hark! The loud celestial hymn
Angel choirs above are raising;
Cherubim and Seraphim,
In unceasing chorus praising,
Fill the Heav'ns with sweet accord:
Holy, holy, holy Lord.

Holy Father, Holy Son,
Holy Spirit, Three we name Thee,
While in essence only One,
Undivided God we claim Thee,
And adoring bend the knee,
While we own the mystery.

Or:

The Divine Praises

Blessed be God.

Blessed be his Holy Name.

Blessed be Jesus Christ, true God and true man.

Blessed be the Name of Jesus.

Blessed be his Most Sacred Heart.

Blessed be his Most Precious Blood.

Blessed be Jesus in the most Holy Sacrament of the Altar.

Blessed be the Holy Spirit, the Paraclete.

Blessed be the great Mother of God, Mary, most holy.

Blessed be her holy and Immaculate Conception.

Blessed be her glorious Assumption.

Blessed be the name of Mary, Virgin and Mother.

Blessed be Saint Joseph, her most chaste Spouse.

Blessed be God in his angels and in his saints.

✠ ✠ ✠ ✠ ✠ ✠ ✠ ✠

God is love and he loves us. That is the heart of the Christian faith.

—Saint André Bessette

✠ ✠ ✠ ✠ ✠ ✠ ✠ ✠

✣ II ✣
Daily Meditation

MEDITATION HAS always held a privileged place in the life of Holy Cross religious. In the *1855 Exercises*, Father Moreau emphasized "the necessity of meditation as one of the acts most essential to our religious life." Later he wrote, "Our meditation determines the entire day, and without prayer and silence we grow negligent in the service of God" (*Circular Letter 136*). Echoing his perspectives, our Constitutions indicate that "each of us needs the nourishment of at least one-half hour of quiet prayer daily" (*Constitution* 3:30). Father Moreau's wise counsels continue to be a support and guide for our spiritual life.

"Meditation is the prayer par excellence where God speaks to our heart, and our heart speaks to God without words. Without meditation, no one will ever be a good religious" (*Circular Letter 96*).

32. PRAYER BEFORE MEDITATION

Lord God,
I firmly believe that you are here,
that you see me, that you hear me.
I adore you with profound reverence.
I beg your pardon for my sins,
and the grace to make this time of prayer fruitful.
May Our Lady of Sorrows and Saint Joseph
    intercede for me.
May the Most Sacred Heart of Jesus have mercy on
    me.

33. AT THE BEGINNING OF MEDITATION

Come, Holy Spirit, fill the hearts of your faithful
and enkindle in them the fire of your love.
Send forth your Spirit and they shall be created.
    —*And you shall renew the face of the earth.*

Let us pray.

O God,
you teach the hearts of the faithful
by the light of the Holy Spirit.
Grant that by the gift of the same Spirit

we may be truly wise and ever rejoice in his
  consolation.
Through Christ our Lord.
Amen.

---

34. Prayers before Reading Scripture

I
(Saint Jerome)

O Lord,
you have given us your word
for a light to shine upon our path.
Grant us so to meditate on that word,
and to follow its teaching,
that we may find in it the light that shines
more and more until the perfect day.
We ask this through Christ our Lord.

II
(Thomas à Kempis)

Let not your word, O Lord,
become a judgment upon us:
that we hear it and do it not;
that we know it and love it not;
that we believe it and obey it not.
You live and reign with the Father and the Holy
  Spirit, world without end.
Amen.

35. TO MARY IMMACULATE

O Mary Immaculate, faithful adorer of the Father,
Mother most admirable of the Son, Spouse of the
    Holy Spirit,
inspire within me the same sentiments that were
    yours while pondering the revealed mysteries
    which you treasured in your heart.
Grant that I may ever live in union with your Son,
    my Savior,
together with all who, by meditation, give honor to
    the most Holy Trinity.
Amen.

36. PRAYER AFTER MEDITATION

I thank you, my God,
for the good resolutions, affections, and inspirations
that you have communicated to me in this
    meditation.
I beg your help in putting them into effect.
May Our Lady of Sorrows and Saint Joseph
    intercede for me.
May the Most Sacred Heart of Jesus have mercy on
    me.

37. O Jesus, Living in Mary
(Jean-Jacques Olier, S.S.)

O Jesus, living in Mary,
come and live in your servants, in the spirit of
    holiness,
in the fullness of your power, in the perfection of
    your ways,
in the truth of your virtues, in the communion of
    your mysteries.
Rule over every adverse power in your Spirit for the
    glory of the Father.
Amen.

38. *Suscipe*
(Saint Ignatius of Loyola)

Take, Lord, and receive all my liberty, my memory,
my understanding, and my entire will,
all that I have and possess.
You have given all to me; to you, O Lord, I now
    return it.
All is yours; dispose of me wholly according to your
    will.

Give me only your love and your grace, for this is
    enough for me.

---

39. SERENITY PRAYER
(Reinhold Niebuhr)

God,
grant me the serenity to accept the things I cannot
    change,
courage to change the things I can,
and wisdom to know the difference,
living one day at a time, enjoying one moment at a
    time,
accepting hardship as the pathway to peace.
Taking as Jesus did this sinful world as it is,
not as I would have it, trusting that he will make all
    things right
if I surrender to his will,
that I may be reasonably happy in this life
and supremely happy with him forever in the next.
Amen.

✣ ✣ ✣ ✣ ✣ ✣ ✣ ✣

The union which recollection establishes between God and our souls will strengthen each one of us in our vocation.

—**Blessed Basil Moreau** (*Circular Letter 134*)

✣ ✣ ✣ ✣ ✣ ✣ ✣ ✣

✦ III ✦
Particular Examen

PARTICULAR EXAMEN is an important practice within Sulpician spirituality, and especially Ignatian spirituality, as a valuable tool for self-knowledge and continuing spiritual growth. Having been attracted to and influenced by both Sulpician and Ignatian spiritualities, Father Moreau highly recommended this practice to the religious of Holy Cross.

Basically, Father Moreau follows the five points for the Examen as they are presented in the *Spiritual Exercises* of Saint Ignatius of Loyola. He adds a distinctive character, however, by associating the five points with the five wounds of Jesus on the Cross. This Examen is done meditatively before a crucifix.

40. ORDER OF EXAMEN

Opening Prayer

(Jean-Jacques Olier, S.S.)

Jesus living in Mary!
Come and live in us by the Spirit of holiness, the
    fullness of your power,
the perfection of your ways, the truth of your
    virtues,
and the communication of your mysteries.
Triumph over all hostile powers by your Spirit,
for the glory of God.
Amen.

Short Reading

Each of the following readings, taken from the
Constitutions, *may be used in the course of the week as*
indicated. Other passages may be chosen.

Monday

"We wished to abandon all to follow Christ. We
learned in time that we still had it within ourselves
to hold back. We wish to be wholehearted, yet we
are hesitant. Still, like the first disciples we know
that he will draw us along and reinforce our loyalties
if we yield to him." (1:8)

Tuesday

"The Lord Jesus was crucified. But the Father raised him to glory, and Christ breathed his Spirit into his people, the church. Dying and rising with him in baptism, his followers are sent to continue his mission, to hasten along the kingdom." (2:10)

Wednesday

"Our mission is the Lord's and so is the strength for it. We turn to him in prayer that he will clasp us more firmly to himself and use our hands and wits to do the work that only he can do." (2:20)

Thursday

"Beyond the liturgy that convokes us into church and congregation, there is the prayer we each must offer to the Father quietly and alone. We contemplate the living God, offering ourselves to be drawn into his love and learning to take that same love to heart." (3:30)

Friday

"We accept the Lord's call to pledge ourselves publicly and perpetually as members of the Congregation of Holy Cross by the vows of consecrated celibacy, poverty, and obedience. Great is the mystery and meaning of these vows. . . . We wish thus to live in the image of Jesus who was sent in love to announce God's rule and who beckons us to follow him." (5:43)

Saturday

"The Lord Jesus loved us and gave up his life for us. Few of us will be called to die the way he died. Yet all of us must lay down our lives with him and for him. If we would be faithful to the gospel we must take up our cross daily and follow him." (8:112)

Sunday

"Jesus entered into the pain and death that sin inflicts. He accepted the torment but gave us joy in return. We whom he has sent to minister amid the same sin and pain must know that we too shall find the cross and the hope it promises. The face of every human being who suffers is for us the face of Jesus who mounted the cross to take the sting out of death. Ours must be the same cross and the same hope." (8:114)

Examen

Wound of the Right Hand
(Thank God for benefits received)

I adore you, O God, and give thanks to you for all your benefits. I am grateful for the graces you have given so freely to your Incarnate Son, to his Mother so full of love, to all the saints, and to all people. I am especially grateful for those graces you have given to me: the gift of my creation, my faith, my vocation in Holy Cross, and for infinite other graces. As an expression of my gratitude, I offer to you the praises of the Church, the merits of your Son, Jesus Christ, my Savior, and the precious blood that flowed from his hands on the Cross.

Wound of the Left Hand
(Ask God for the light necessary to know my faults)

O God dwelling within my heart! I ask you, through the precious blood that flowed from the hands of your Son, give me the grace to know, detest, and correct my faults. By that grace and on the day of judgment, may I be placed not on the left but on the right hand of the Divine and Just Judge.

Wound of the Right Foot
(Examine my conscience)

Lord, I am far from the path of perfection so clearly marked for me by the Blood of Jesus Christ! How many are the faults I have committed this day!

At this point, examine one's thoughts, words, deeds, and omissions.

Wound of the Left Foot
(Ask forgiveness for my sins)

O my God, I have sinned in your presence. With all my heart, I am sorry for having sinned, for you

are infinitely good and holy. I have loved objects
of no lasting value more than you. I have pre-
ferred them to my eternal and greatest good. I am
resolved to love you more than all the creatures of
this world. I detest my sins because they displease
you. I hold to the feet of your Son and ask you,
by his wounds, let him say to me even as he did to
Mary Magdalene, "Your sins are forgiven." With
this hope, I place myself entirely within Jesus'
wounds, in his merciful heart. I hope your goodness will grant me forgiveness through the merits
of Jesus' passion. Let your face shine upon me and
have mercy on me.

Wound of the Heart of Jesus
(Renew my daily resolutions)

Jesus! God of love, from this time forward, I
promise to respond fully to the desires of your
heart, pierced on the Cross for my salvation. I will
continue to correct all my faults and negligences.
I choose not to sin again, not even in the least
things. Confirm in me these resolutions and in the
others I have made this day, through the graces of
Jesus' blood which poured out from his heart. I
offer all this to you, in atonement with your life,
your passion, and your death. Amen.

*Particular Examen concludes with the Hail Mary, in
honor of Our Lady of Holy Cross.*

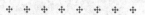

People who suffer have something to offer to God. When they succeed in enduring their suffering, that is a daily miracle.

—**Saint André Bessette**

✤ I V ✤
Sacrament of
Reconciliation

LIFELONG FORMATION is lifelong growth. As a daily aid for self-knowledge and self-governance, the examination of conscience allows us to find how we succeed or fall short in both our common life and our mission. A grace more powerful still is given in appropriately frequent sacramental confession, whereby each of us opens his conscience to the Lord, to the Lord's minister and to himself and there finds reconciliation with his neighbors and pardon from the Lord, who gave his life lest any of us be lost to him. (*Constitution 6:77*)

41. PRAYER BEFORE EXAMINATION OF CONSCIENCE

O my God,
behold me, a poor sinner who humbly comes
    before you seeking your infinite mercy.
Filled with confusion for my excesses, I wish to
    return to you.
Unworthy as I am, I dare to raise my voice in
    supplication for your infinite mercy.
May your heart, O God, be open to my prayer!
I beg you, O God, that I may know my heart,
    that I may thoroughly know myself.
Grant that I may see all of my sins, their number,
    their malice,
and their enormity, so that I may be reconciled
    perfectly with you.

O Holy Spirit, source of light,
dissipate the darkness that blinds me;
enlighten my mind that I may know all of my
    faults.
Soften my heart, so that I may detest all of my sins.

O Mary, Mother of God and refuge of sinners,
pray for me, a poor sinner, as I place all my
    confidence in you.

42. EXAMINATION OF CONSCIENCE
(based on the Constitutions of the Congregation of Holy Cross)

Constitution 1: God's Call

> *"We wished to abandon all to follow Christ. We learned in time that we still had it within ourselves to hold back. We wish to be wholehearted yet we are hesitant. Still, like the first disciples we know that he will draw us along and reinforce our loyalties if we yield to him." (1:8)*

In what special ways have I made a concerted effort to give of myself wholeheartedly to God and to the mission of Holy Cross?

When were the times when I felt myself hesitant or holding back? What is there in my life or ministry that presently prevents me from total abandonment to God's will?

Are there times when I depended more upon my own power as opposed to the power of God's fidelity? Have I sought God above everything else, or have I put other things (i.e., ambition, friendships, comfort, etc.) before God?

Have I neglected to use my gifts and tal*e* the good of the community?

Constitution 2: Mission

> *"Our efforts, which are his, reach out to the*
> *afflicted and in a preferential way to the poor*
> *and oppressed. . . .We stand with the poor and*
> *afflicted because only from there can we appeal*
> *as Jesus did for the conversion and deliverance*
> *of all." (2:13)*

Given the circumstances of ministry, in what ways have I neglected to reach out to the poor, oppressed, and afflicted? Have I ever spoken or acted despairingly toward them? Are there times when I have put my own needs before theirs?

Have I failed to pray for those less fortunate, for those who struggle, and for those who seek justice?

> *"There are networks of privilege, prejudice and*
> *power so commonplace that often neither oppres-*
> *sors nor victims are aware of them." (2:14)*

Have I used the status of my religious life or ministry for preferential treatment or for selfish gains? Have I misused my power and authority? How have these actions hurt others? Have I held others in contempt?

What attitudes of mine are rooted in prejudice
    people of a different cultural/ethnic group,

way of thinking, or persuasion? How have I acted on these sinful attitudes?

Have I lied or exaggerated to make myself look good? Have I sought recognition or advancement for my own glory as opposed to the glory of God?

> *"And, as in every work of our mission, we find that we ourselves stand to learn much from those who we are called to teach."* (2:16)

In my living and working with others, do I show them respect by listening to their ideas, thoughts, and opinions?

How has my pride, arrogance, or stubbornness prevented me from learning from those whom I am called to serve? How have I failed to see God in them?

Constitution 3: Prayer

> *"The Lord's supper is the church's foremost gathering for prayer. It is our duty and need to break that bread and share that cup every day unless prevented by serious cause. . . . We find ourselves especially close as a brotherhood when we share this greatest of all table fellowships."* (3:27)

What is my participation in the sacramental life of the Church? Do I make daily Eucharist a priority in my life? For the times that I have missed Mass, was it because of laziness or grave cause?

Do I take the time to prepare myself properly to partake in this "greatest of all table fellowships"? When available, how regularly do I participate in Eucharist with members of my community?

> *"We in Holy Cross also have the need, in some regular rhythm resolved upon in each house, to pray and worship together. It is especially fitting that we join in the two chief hours of the church's daily worship, morning prayer and evening prayer, and that we all free ourselves to take part."* (3:28)

Am I faithful to my community prayer? Do I support my brothers at common prayer by demonstrating a proper deportment and attitude?

> *"We enter thus into the mystery of God who chose to dwell in the midst of his people. His eucharistic presence is the pledge of that. It is especially appropriate then for us to pray in the presence of the reserved eucharist. Each of us needs the nourishment of at least one half-hour of quiet prayer daily. We need as well to assimilate sacred scripture and reflectively to read books on the spiritual life."* (3:30)

Do I reserve at least thirty minutes each day for personal prayer and reflection on the holy scriptures?

Is spiritual reading and spiritual direction a regular discipline in my life?

How do I strengthen, deepen, and show my devotion to the Eucharist? To Mary, our Mother of Sorrows, Saint Joseph, and the Sacred Heart?

> *"Each of us has the need to draw aside from his occupations and preoccupations every year for a retreat of several days of undisturbed prayer and reflection. . . . Likewise, periodic days of recollection refresh our dedication."* (3:31)

Do I give priority to my annual retreat? Do I allow myself enough time for retreat? How often do I take a day away from ministry for personal reflection and prayer? Do I see these times of retreat more as a burden than as a value?

Constitution 4: Brotherhood

> *"In our common life we give an immediate and tangible expression to what we profess through our vows: in the local community we share the companionship, the goods and the united efforts of our celibacy, poverty and obedience."* (4:34)

Do I actively participate in the life of my local community? Do I respect the agreed upon rules of living in my local community, and am I faithful to my duties? Do I show proper stewardship of common goods and funds?

Do I diminish community union by engaging or promoting gossip? Have I taken pleasure in the failures of my brothers?

Have I in any way contributed to a poor witness of religious life? Could my words or actions have been interpreted by others as scandalous?

> *"Our local communities should be generous in continuing our tradition of hospitality to confreres, to those who labor with us, to our relatives and neighbors, and to the poor, especially those who have no one to have them in." (4:40)*

Am I hospitable to guests? Am I generous with my time, solicitude, and conversation? Do I show the same reverence to all guests, or to only those I know or like?

> *"Thus it is part of our lives to extend brotherly correction and apology to one another and in frank yet discreet ways to reconcile. Our very failures can then be transformed by God's grace into closer comradeship." (4:41)*

Have I intentionally hurt others in community through my words or actions? Has my humor been unkind and at the expense of others? Have I actively sought reconciliation when needed?

Am I charitable and forgiving of those who have hurt me? Have I harbored grudges, resentment, or hatred for others? Have I been vengeful?

Do I reach out charitably in prayer and action to those who are sick, troubled, sorrowful, or frequently absent?

Constitution 5: Consecration and Commitment

"By our vow of celibacy we commit ourselves to seek union with God in lifelong chastity, forgoing forever marriage and parenthood for the sake of the kingdom. We also promise loyalty, companionship and affection to our confreres in Holy Cross. Openness and discipline in prayer, personal asceticism, compassionate service, and love given and received in community are important supports toward generous living of this commitment." (5:47)

Do I show warmth and compassion in my relationships with others, or am I distant, aloof, and insular?

Is my primary source of support for my religious life and ministry the brothers with whom I live or those outside of the community? Have I spoke negatively of my brothers to those outside of the community?

Have I engaged in unhealthy behaviors that are inconsistent with vowed celibate chastity? Have I respected my body and the bodies of others? How often have I engaged in impure thoughts, pornography, and questionable media?

> *"By our vow of poverty we submit to the direction of community authority in our use and disposition of property, for we commit ourselves to hold our goods in common and to share them as brothers. All remuneration for our services, all income, gifts and benefits are ours to share or dispose of as a community."* (5:48)

Am I generous in sharing my time, talents, and possessions with others? Is my personal lifestyle, in its tastes and preferences, reflective of simplicity and consecrated poverty?

Do I depend solely upon community funds for my personal needs, or do I seek outside sources of revenue?

Do I accept gifts and other sources of income on my behalf or on behalf of the community?

> *"By our vow of obedience we commit ourselves to adhere faithfully to the decisions of those in Holy Cross according to the constitutions; we owe obedience to the Pope as well."* (5:50)

Have I put my own choices, needs, and preferences before that of the community?

Do I respect, support, and pray for those who exercise leadership and authority in the Church, including the pope and the Congregation?

Have I been jealous or envious of those in authority?

Constitution 6: Formation and Transformation

> *"Our experience in Holy Cross is demanding. It is joyful as well. . . . If we delight in our vocation, we will share it with others."* (6:60)

Do I live my vocation in a way that it is attractive to others? Am I welcoming, hospitable, and inviting?

> *"It is commonly imagined that our formation is most extensive when we are beginners. But often our most radical formative experiences come upon us when we are well into adulthood. Indeed, we can better grasp and accept profound self-scrutiny, the questioning of our established assumptions and ambitions, and*

> *deepening initiation into Christ when we have walked the path of adult experience and responsibility. Programs of continuing renewal in the community are one very helpful way of sharing that lifelong formation." (6:76)*

Do I take time to nurture and to renew my vocation to religious life in Holy Cross?

Do I regularly examine my conscience? Am I faithful to the sacrament of Reconciliation? Do I seek the help, personal or professional, of others when I struggle or am in crisis?

Constitution 7: Authority and Responsibility

> *"There can be no community among us unless our common life and mission are governed by deliberations and decisions that draw us all towards a unity of thought, sentiment and action. To those deliberations and decisions we are all obligated as men pledged to obedience both to contribute and to respond." (7:80)*

Do I actively participate in community decision-making processes when asked or required, or do I choose to forego my voice?

Have my words or actions uncharitably contributed to disunity, disparity, or a diminished spirit in community?

If I am able, do I show my shared responsibility in Holy Cross by making efforts to attend community funerals, professions, jubilees, and other celebrations or gatherings?

> *"We must be responsible—each of us—for the conformity of our lives to the gospel and for the harmony of our ministries with the mission of Christ. In chapter or in council or as individuals, we owe it to our confreres to enter into frank and respectful exchange about the decisions that are to be taken which affect us all. The Spirit of the Lord may choose any of us to speak the truths we all need to hear. Our vow of obedience itself obliges each of us take appropriate responsibility for the common good." (7:81)*

Am I faithful to my participation at house chapters? At such occasions, do I tell the truth without blame or judgment? Am I open to thoughts and opinions of others?

Is my concern for the common good of the community, or is it for my own needs and will? In others words, do I seek my will or the will of the community?

In what areas of my common life have I neglected to assume responsibility?

Constitution 8: The Cross, Our Hope

> *"But we do not grieve as men without hope, for Christ the Lord has risen to die no more. He has taken us into the mystery and the grace of this life that springs up from death. If we, like him encounter and accept suffering in our discipleship, we will move without awkwardness among others who suffer. We must be men with hope to bring."* (8:118)

Are there times when I have failed to recognize the value of redemptive suffering and given into cynicism and despair? In times of suffering, do I focus solely on myself and my own needs?

Am I a hopeful presence in community and ministry? When have I failed to bring a witness of Gospel-centered hope to those whom I encountered?

43. PRAYER BEFORE CONFESSION

O my God,
be in my heart and on my lips
that I may make a sincere and full confession of my
    sins.
Be in the mind and in the words of my confessor
that he may see the depth of my weak humanity,

and that he may offer me the compassionate and
  healing balm of the divine Physician, Jesus
  Christ,
who alone can heal and save.
Amen.

44. Prayer for Contrition

Behold me, O God,
as I acknowledge my sins.
I detest them with all my heart.
I am sincerely sorry for having offended a God
  so deserving of my love.
You have shed your blood for me, and I have been
  ungrateful.
I humbly implore your pardon,
and I beg of you, by the goodness you have so
  often shown me,
to grant me the grace to do penance for my sins.

45. Act of Contrition

My God,
I am sorry for my sins with all my heart.
In choosing to do wrong

and failing to do good,
I have sinned against you
whom I should love above all things.
I firmly intend, with your help,
to do penance,
to sin no more,
and to avoid whatever leads me to sin.
Our Savior Jesus Christ
suffered and died for us.
In his name, my God, have mercy.

✣ ✣ ✣ ✣ ✣ ✣ ✣ ✣ ✣

*God will draw good from evil, and these crosses will be
the means of salvation for many.*

—Blessed Basil Moreau (*Circular
Letter 45* to the Sisters)

✣ ✣ ✣ ✣ ✣ ✣ ✣ ✣ ✣

✤ V ✤
Stations of the Cross

FATHER MOREAU has written that "no moment in the history of the world is so memorable, so awesome and moving, as the moment when the cross of Jesus Christ was raised on Calvary. And when the cross with its precious Burden was finally in its place, dominating the horizon as the mysterious Sign of divine justice and mercy, the crowd surged toward it.... For the moment, this movement was one of hatred, but it was presently to be a surge of love whose great waves were to beat against this rock and his holy Cross until the end of time." (*Daily Meditations*)

46. STATIONS OF THE CROSS (I)

In the name of the Father, and of the Son, and of the Holy Spirit. Amen.

Reading from the Writings of Basil Moreau

"In following Jesus we are sure of reaching heaven. To follow him, however, it is necessary to deny ourselves and carry the cross. If we carry our cross after Jesus we will live. Life is in the cross and no place else. But we must not only take up the cross, we must carry it with courage. If we drag it after us, if we abandon it after having taken it up, if we trample it under foot, it will not save us. Let us follow the path that Jesus has walked and we will arrive at a happy eternity." (*Conference*)

First Station: Jesus Is Condemned to Death

We adore you, O Christ, and we praise you.
  —*For by your holy Cross you have redeemed the world.*

Scripture

"But he was silent and did not answer. Again the high priest asked him, 'Are you the Messiah, the

Son of the Blessed One?' Jesus said, 'I am.'" (Mk 14:61–62)

Constitutions

"Whether it be unfair treatment, fatigue or frustration at work, a lapse of health, tasks beyond talents, seasons of loneliness, bleakness in prayer, the aloofness of friends, or whether it be the sadness of having inflicted any of this on others . . . there will be dying to do on our way to the Father." (8:117)

Basil Moreau

"Now, Jesus, comes the blessed day you had anticipated for thirty-three years. You would now offer yourself as a victim by the hand of the executioner. This was where you would begin to pass the work of our redemption. This is the hour when your enemies, inspired by the forces of evil, waited with great impatience to calm their rage and this would announce the reconciliation of heaven with earth." (*Christian Meditations*)

Lord Jesus, your Cross is our glory.
—*Your Cross is our only hope.*

Second Station: Jesus Takes Up the Cross

We adore you, O Christ, and we praise you.
—*For by your holy Cross you have redeemed the world.*

Scripture

"Now it was the day of Preparation for the Passover; and it was about noon. [Pilate] said to the Jews, 'Here is your King!' They cried out, 'Away with him! Away with him! Crucify him!' Pilate asked them, 'Shall I crucify your King?' The chief priests answered, 'We have no king but the emperor.' Then he handed him over to them to be crucified. So they took Jesus, and carrying the cross by himself, he went out to what is called The Place of the Skull, which in Hebrew is called Golgotha." (Jn 19:14–17)

Constitutions

"We must be men with hope to bring. There is no failure the Lord's love cannot reverse, no humiliation he cannot exchange for blessings, no anger he cannot dissolve, no routine he cannot transfigure. All is swallowed up in victory. It remains for us to find how even the cross can be borne as a gift." (8:118)

Basil Moreau

"See now the love of Jesus' heart for you in order to render him the homage of your own. Not content with being made man for you by the incarnation, your brother in his birth, your Savior in his circumcision, your light in his epiphany, he wished to abase himself to the lowest degree, to embrace the most obscure, humble and difficult way of life, to condemn himself to the most painful labors, in a word, to support all the privations attached to the poor and the disinherited classes of society." (*Christian Meditations*)

Lord Jesus, your Cross is our glory.
—*Your Cross is our only hope.*

Third Station: Jesus Falls the First Time

We adore you, O Christ, and we praise you.
—*For by your holy Cross you have redeemed the world.*

Scripture

"Now after John was arrested, Jesus came to Galilee, proclaiming the good news of God, and saying, 'The time is fulfilled, and the kingdom of God has come near; repent, and believe in the good news.'" (Mk 1:14–15)

Constitutions

"Jesus entered into the pain and death that sin inflicts. He accepted the torment but gave us joy in return. We whom he has sent to minister amid the same sin and pain must know that we too shall find the cross and the hope it promises. The face of every human being who suffers is for us the face of Jesus who mounted the cross to take the sting out of death. Ours must be the same cross and the same hope." (8:114)

Basil Moreau

"It seems as though, in the midst of our trials, God wanted to remind us constantly of the cross of Jesus Christ, in order to encourage us to carry our own. For these crosses become heavier daily, even though we always look upon them as hopeful signs for the future." (*Annals of Holy Cross*)

Lord Jesus, your Cross is our glory.
   —*Your Cross is our only hope.*

Fourth Station: Jesus Meets His Mother

We adore you, O Christ, and we praise you.
   —*For by your holy Cross you have redeemed the world.*

Scripture

"Meanwhile, standing near the cross of Jesus were his mother, and his mother's sister, Mary the wife of Clopas, and Mary Magdalene. When Jesus saw his mother and the disciple whom he loved standing beside her, he said to his mother, 'Woman, here is your son.' Then he said to the disciple, 'Here is your mother.' And from that hour the disciple took her into his own home." (Jn 19:25–27)

Constitutions

"There stood by the cross of Jesus his mother Mary, who knew grief and was a Lady of Sorrows. She is our special patroness, a woman who bore much she could not understand and who stood fast. To her many sons and daughters, whose devotions ought to bring them often to her side, she tells much of this daily cross and its daily hope." (8:120)

Basil Moreau

"Mary's heart was the most tender and most loving heart imaginable, after the heart of the Savior himself. We understand a bit of the emotion called motherly love, this love of a mother for the children she has brought to life. Motherly love leads her always to think about them and work to assure their happiness. This is but a faint picture of what Mary feels for all people, and the love she bears for us, since she became our mother and she adopted us as her children." (*Sermon*)

Lord Jesus, your Cross is our glory.
　—*Your Cross is our only hope.*

Fifth Station: Simon of Cyrene Helps Jesus to Carry the Cross

We adore you, O Christ, and we praise you.
—*For by your holy Cross you have redeemed the world.*

Scripture

"As they led him away, they seized a man, Simon of Cyrene, who was coming from the country, and they laid the cross on him, and made him carry it behind Jesus." (Lk 23:26)

Constitutions

"Our calling is to serve the Lord Jesus in mission not as independent individuals but in a brotherhood. . . . We grow close to one another as brothers by living together in community. If we do not love the brothers whom we see, then we cannot love the God whom we have not seen." (4:33–34)

Basil Moreau

"I understand, my good friend, how crushing your responsibilities are and how sorely you are in need of grace, without which you would collapse under them. But who would be so bold as to run away from such a burden when God himself has laid it upon your shoulders?" (*Personal Letter*)

Lord Jesus, your Cross is our glory.
—*Your Cross is our only hope.*

Sixth Station: Veronica Wipes the Face of Jesus

We adore you, O Christ, and we praise you.
—*For by your holy Cross you have redeemed the world.*

Scripture

"Little children, I am with you only a little longer. You will look for me; and as I said to the Jews so now I say to you, 'Where I am going, you cannot come.' I give you a new commandment, that you love one another. Just as I have loved you, you also should love one another. By this everyone will know that you are my disciples, if you have love for one another." (Jn 13:33–35)

Constitutions

"It is essential to our mission that we strive to abide so attentively together that people will observe: 'See how they love one another.' We will then be a sign in an alienated world: men who have, for love of their Lord, become closest neighbors, trustworthy friends, brothers." (4:42)

Basil Moreau

"I sympathize with your sufferings, my dear daughter. But do not lose sight of the fact that this is now the omen of a future full of blessings, and that the cross alone can sanctify us, save us, and make us useful for the salvation of others." (*Personal Letter*)

Lord Jesus, your Cross is our glory.
　　—*Your Cross is our only hope.*

Seventh Station: Jesus Falls the Second Time

We adore you, O Christ, and we praise you.
　　—*For by your holy Cross you have redeemed the world.*

Scripture

"Simon Peter said to him, 'Lord, where are you going?' Jesus answered, 'Where I am going, you cannot follow me now; but you will follow afterwards.' Peter said to him, 'Lord, why can I not follow you now? I will lay down my life for you.' Jesus answered, 'Will you lay down your life for me? Very truly, I tell you, before the cock crows, you will have denied me three times.'" (Jn 13:36–38)

Constitutions

"It is not merely we who pray, but his Spirit who prays in us. And we who busy ourselves in announcing the Lord's kingdom need to come back often enough and sit at his feet and listen still more closely." (3:32)

Basil Moreau

"Jesus Christ is pleased to test his work; only a religious spirit which understands the power of his cross can sustain our courage in the midst of trials. Happy indeed are we if we know how to profit by them and to understand the unspeakable advantage of becoming more and more conformed to the image of the Divine Christ crucified. For those who live by faith the cross is a treasure more valuable than gold and precious stones. If we were truly worthy of our vocation, far from dreading these crosses, we would be more eager to accept them than receive a relic of the very wood which our Savior sanctified by his blood. Let us not allow ourselves, then, to be discouraged by trials, no matter how numerous or bitter they may be." (*Circular Letter*)

Lord Jesus, your Cross is our glory.
　—*Your Cross is our only hope.*

Eighth Station: Jesus Meets the Women of Jerusalem

We adore you, O Christ, and we praise you.
—*For by your holy Cross you have redeemed the world.*

Scripture

"A great number of the people followed him, and among them were women who were beating their breasts and wailing for him. But Jesus turned to them and said, 'Daughters of Jerusalem, do not weep for me, but weep for yourselves and for your children.'" (Lk 23:27–28)

Constitutions

"But we do not grieve as men without hope, for Christ the Lord has risen to die no more. He has taken us into the mystery and grace of this life that springs from death. If we, like him, encounter and accept suffering in our discipleship, we will move without awkwardness among others who suffer." (8:118)

Basil Moreau

"Behold our cross. Human life is only a long way of the cross. It is not necessary to enter the chapel or the church to run over the various stations. The way of the cross is everywhere and we walk along it every day in spite of ourselves and often unknown to us. After all, what else should we desire since there is no other way to reach heaven. Also, there are many consolations for those who carry their cross with generosity. If we try a road other than that of the cross we will be lost and, in addition, we will meet with still heavier crosses. If we avoid one cross, which at times is possible in a religious community, we will certainly meet with another, ordinarily much heavier than the one we avoided." (*Conference*)

Lord Jesus, your Cross is our glory.
—*Your Cross is our only hope.*

Ninth Station: Jesus Falls the Third Time

We adore you, O Christ, and we praise you.
—*For by your holy Cross you have redeemed the world.*

Scripture

"Then he took the twelve aside and said to them, 'See, we are going up to Jerusalem, and everything that is written about the Son of Man by the prophets will be accomplished. For he will be handed over to the Gentiles; and he will be mocked and insulted and spat upon. After they have flogged him, they will kill him, and on the third day he will rise again.' But they understood nothing about all these things; in fact, what he said was hidden from them, and they did not grasp what was said." (Lk 18:31–34)

Constitutions

"When we do serve him faithfully, it is our work that rouses us to prayer. The abundance of his gifts, dismay over our ingratitude, and the crying needs of our neighbors—all this is brought home to us in our ministry and it draws us into prayer." (4:26)

Basil Moreau

"There are, doubtless, a goodly number of crosses for one year, not to mention those which from time to time are provided by ill will, lying, and slander. Far from complaining of these trials, we must learn to love them, for if we bear them as we should they are worth their weight in gold. I do not know what new crosses await us during the coming year. Whatever they may be, let us not forget that the heaviest crosses contribute most to the general good of our work and to the welfare of each one of us." (*Circular Letter*)

Lord Jesus, your Cross is our glory.
—*Your Cross is our only hope.*

Tenth Station: Jesus Is Stripped of His Clothes

We adore you, O Christ, and we praise you.
  —*For by your holy Cross you have redeemed the world*.

Scripture

"And when they came to a place called Golgotha (which means Place of a Skull), they offered him wine to drink, mixed with gall; but when he tasted it, he would not drink it. And when they had crucified him, they divided his clothes among themselves by casting lots; then they sat down there and kept watch over him." (Mt 27:33–36)

Constitutions

"The mission is not simple, for the impoverishments we would relieve are not simple. There are networks of privilege, prejudice, and power so commonplace that often neither oppressors nor victims are aware of them. We must be aware and also understanding by reason of fellowship with the impoverished and by reason of patient learning. For the kingdom to come in this world, disciples must have the competence to see and the courage to act." (2:14)

Basil Moreau

"Try, then, to become perfect copies of the Divine Model, and nothing will ever shake your vocation. Not only will you carry whatever crosses you encounter in accomplishing the duties of your holy state, but you will love these crosses. Yes, you will even desire them and, after the example of our Lord, will choose them in preference to everything else." (*Circular Letter*)

Lord Jesus, your Cross is our glory.
—*Your Cross is our only hope.*

Eleventh Station: Jesus Is Nailed to the Cross

We adore you, O Christ, and we praise you.
—*For by your holy Cross you have redeemed the world.*

Scripture

"It was nine o'clock in the morning when they crucified him. The inscription of the charge against him read, 'The King of the Jews.' And with him they crucified two bandits, one on his right and one on his left." (Mk 15:25–27)

Constitutions

"To struggle for justice and meet only stubbornness, to try to rally those who have despaired, to stand by the side of misery we cannot relieve, to preach the Lord to those who have little faith or who do not wish to hear of him . . . our ministry will hint to us of Jesus' suffering for us." (8:115)

Basil Moreau

"The second precept concerning the love of your neighbor is like the first because the legitimate love of your neighbor comes under the love of God and is referred entirely to him. Your neighbor is not the motive nor the end of the love you should have for him. Let him be good or bad, friend or enemy, grateful or ungrateful, let him be personally deserving of love, you should love him for God, with regard to God, because God wishes it, commands it, and has written this law in your heart. The rule for loving your neighbor is to love him as you love yourself. This signifies, not an equality of sentiment, but an equality of duties; that is, you must treat your neighbor as you have the right to wish to be treated." (*Christian Meditations*)

Lord Jesus, your Cross is our glory.
—*Your Cross is our only hope.*

Twelfth Station: Jesus Dies on the Cross

We adore you, O Christ, and we praise you.
—*For by your holy Cross you have redeemed the world.*

Scripture

"It was now about noon, and darkness came over the whole land until three in the afternoon, while the sun's light failed; and the curtain of the temple was torn in two. Then Jesus, crying with a loud voice, said, 'Father, into your hands I commend my spirit.' Having said this, he breathed his last." (Lk 23:44–46)

Constitutions

"If we drink the cup each of us is poured and given, we servants will fare no better than our master. But if we shirk the cross, gone too will be our hope. It is in fidelity to what we once pledged that we will find the dying and rising equally assured." (8:121)

Basil Moreau

"This is the way, Jesus, you gave your life for your sheep like the Good Shepherd. Thus you give us the most touching example of patience, forgiveness of injuries, resignation and love. After having given us your body as our food, your mother Mary as our mother, the Church for our country in this world, and heaven as our eternal dwelling place, you departed to return to your Father." (*Christian Meditations*)

Lord Jesus, your Cross is our glory.
	—*Your Cross is our only hope.*

Thirteenth Station: Jesus Is Removed from the Cross

We adore you, O Christ, and we praise you.

—*For by your holy Cross you have redeemed the world.*

Scripture

"Since it was the day of Preparation, the Jews did not want the bodies left on the cross during the Sabbath, especially because that Sabbath was a day of great solemnity. So they asked Pilate to have the legs of the crucified men broken and the bodies removed. Then the soldiers came and broke the legs of the first and of the other who had been crucified with him. But when they came to Jesus and saw that he was already dead, they did not break his legs. Instead, one of the soldiers pierced his side with a spear, and at once blood and water came out." (Jn 19:31–34)

Constitutions

"The footsteps of those men who called us to walk in their company left deep prints, as of men carrying heavy burdens. But they did not trudge; they strode. For they had the hope." (8:122)

Basil Moreau

"Mary received your lifeless body in her arms, let your body rest on her knees, and then she washed

your bloody wounds with her tears. Permit me
to offer you this day the homage she gave to you
then, that it may make up for the insufficiency of
my adoration, my compassion, and my gratitude."
(*Christian Meditations*)

Lord Jesus, your Cross is our glory.
—*Your Cross is our only hope.*

Fourteenth Station: Jesus Is Placed in the Tomb

We adore you, O Christ, and we praise you.
—*For by your holy Cross you have redeemed the world.*

Scripture

"After these things, Joseph of Arimathea, who was
a disciple of Jesus, though a secret one because of
his fear of the Jews, asked Pilate to let him take
away the body of Jesus. Pilate gave him permission;
so he came and removed his body. Nicodemus,
who had at first come to Jesus by night, also came,
bringing a mixture of myrrh and aloes, weighing
about a hundred pounds. They took the body of
Jesus and wrapped it with the spices in linen cloths,
according to the burial custom of the Jews. Now
there was a garden in the place where he was crucified, and in the garden there was a new tomb in
which no one had ever been laid. And so, because

it was the Jewish day of Preparation, and the tomb was nearby, they laid Jesus there." (Jn 19:38–42)

Constitutions

"The cross was constantly before the eyes of Basil Moreau, whose motto for his congregation was *Spes Unica*. The cross was to be 'Our Only Hope.'" (8:113)

Basil Moreau

"I bow to the sacred tomb wherein was enclosed my Savior, precious cloth covered his adorable face, venerated shroud within which the body of Jesus was wrapped, and on which it left its wounded imprint. I unite myself with the angels who guarded you, and with them venerate your head crowned with the marks of the thorns, your side opened by the thrust of the spear, your pierced hands and feet. Do me the honor and the grace to bury yourself in my heart. Let me anoint you with the perfumes of devotion, the myrrh of sanctification, the aloes of prayer, that my heart may also have the fragrance of Christ." (*Christian Meditations*)

Lord Jesus, your Cross is our glory.
—*Your Cross is our only hope.*

The following may be omitted, in which case one proceeds to the concluding prayer below.

Conclusion: The Resurrection

We adore you, O Christ, and we praise you.
—*For by your holy Cross you have redeemed the world.*

Scripture

"But on the first day of the week, at early dawn, they came to the tomb, taking the spices that they had prepared. They found the stone rolled away from the tomb, but when they went in, they did not find the body." (Lk 24:1–3)

Constitutions

"It is the Lord Jesus calling us, 'Come. Follow me.'" (8:123)

Basil Moreau

"Jesus does not have only the appearance of one raised from the dead, but he lives a life entirely different from the first life. This is to teach us that everything needs to be renewed in our lives, our thoughts, desires, words and actions. Not only does he live a new life, but he showed it to his disciples. This is to teach us also to become new people. Lastly, clothed with immortality, he showed us that we must no longer die to grace by sin. Let us adore him here as the Savior of the world, as the head and founder of the Church, to whom the Eternal Father gave all the nations as an inheritance, and to whom he submitted every creature in heaven." (*Christian Meditations*)

Lord Jesus, your Cross is our glory.
—*Your Cross is our only hope.*

Concluding Prayer

Let us pray.

Lord Jesus Christ,
you made this journey to Calvary,
and to your death on the Cross, for love of us
and to show us the way we must follow to be one
    with you.
Forgive us for the times we have not been faithful
    in carrying the Cross.
Accept our love for you as an expression of our
    willingness to make this journey with you
    throughout our lives.
As you have lived and died for us,
we choose to live and die for you,
always united to you.
Hear our prayer and help us.
We ask this in your name, for you are Lord forever
    and ever.
Amen.

✠ ✠ ✠ ✠ ✠ ✠ ✠

We must bear in mind that since our Divine Model remained nailed to the Cross even to his last breath, we too must desire to stay with our cross even to death.
    —Blessed Basil Moreau (*Circular Letter 23*)

✠ ✠ ✠ ✠ ✠ ✠ ✠

47. STATIONS OF THE CROSS (II)

This version of the Stations of the Cross, from *You Have Redeemed the World: Praying the Stations in the Holy Cross Tradition*, edited by Andrew Gawrych, C.S.C., and Kevin Grove, C.S.C., is reprinted with permission (Ave Maria Press, 2010).

Introduction

By his holy Cross, Jesus Christ has redeemed the world. The steps he took on the way to Calvary were not only for you or for me but also for all humanity. The more profoundly we are able to walk these steps with our Lord, the more his passion, death, and resurrection bear fruit in our lives. Jesus' Way of the Cross inspired many early Christians to make a pilgrimage to Jerusalem and follow in his last steps. This practice grew into the devotion of the Stations of the Cross as we know it today. The faithful can now go to their own local church or other place of prayer and make a pilgrimage of prayer and meditation following images that recount Jesus' way to Calvary. And yet, as Blessed Basil Moreau, the saintly founder of Holy Cross wrote, "Human life is like a great Way of the Cross. We do not have to go to the chapel or church to go through the different stations. This Way of the Cross is everywhere and we travel it every day, even in spite of ourselves and without being aware of it." Drawing upon this conviction that we each walk the Way of the Cross in our own lives, the following fourteen stations unite the steps of ordinary people with the steps of Jesus. As we enter into their steps, we are drawn ever more fully into Christ's. The meditations and prayers of these stations are written by members of Holy Cross religious communities from around the world whose lives and mission are rooted in the belief, *Ave Crux, Spes Unica*, "Hail the Cross, Our Only Hope." Praying these stations together, we awaken to a deeper awareness of the transforming power of the Cross and the true hope it brings to us all.

Opening Prayer

In the name of the Father, and of the Son, and of
the Holy Spirit.
—*Amen.*

Lord Jesus,
by your holy Cross you have redeemed the world.
As we retrace your saving steps to Calvary,
reveal to us how your Cross has become
the new tree of life for all creation.
May your mother, Our Lady of Sorrows,
who walked those painful steps with you,
accompany us.
May she guide us along your way that leads
through sacrifice and death to true life.
Make known in our minds and hearts the power of
your Cross, our only hope.
—*Amen.*

First Station: Jesus Is Condemned to Die

We adore you, O Christ, and we praise you.
—*Because by your holy Cross you have redeemed
the world!*

The crowd can be fickle, loving in one breath and
condemning with the next. Today's hero—whether

rock star, candidate, or quarterback—rides into town amidst the din of a million delirious voices shouting hosannas of praise. Yet with any sign of weakness, real or imagined, adulation turns to anger; sweet voices become shrill. Disappointed masses rage in judgment, often destroying the one they so recently adored.

—*Jesus, as our Messiah,*
  you faced the weakness of human power and
  endured torture while offering no resistance.
  Pilate proclaimed your innocence, yet sent you to
    the slaughter.
  Your silent acceptance of that horrific end
  was the full flowering of divine love in our weary
    human flesh.
  Lord Jesus, at times we join our voices in
  adulation of the false gods of our world;
  help us always to turn back again to you.
  In our own moments of suffering,
  may we come to witness to the same love
  you have revealed to us in your passion.

Hail the Cross,
  —*Our only hope.*

Second Station: Jesus Takes Up His Cross

We adore you, O Christ, and we praise you.
>   —*Because by your holy Cross you have redeemed the world!*

There was no way, really, to prepare for the arrival of their first child. Pregnancy was just the beginning. How could someone so small turn everything completely around? Sometimes she could feel so tired and drained. When he had no more to give, more was demanded. Yet when the young parents looked at the eyes and smile of their little one, they knew what the Lord had entrusted to them. There would be no limit to love.

>   —*Lord Jesus,*
>   *you call us to carry our crosses; and you teach us*
>   *how by having done so yourself.*
>   *You chose the Cross. You embraced it.*
>   *You tell us to believe in you and choose with you the*
>   *way of finding new opportunity in challenge,*
>   *love and hope in suffering,*
>   *and even new life in death.*
>   *Work in our lives to transform dead wood into the*
>   *new tree of life.*
>   *Give us your grace and strength so we too may say,*
>   *"Your will be done."*

*Re-create our hearts through the "yes" we offer you
    each day.*

Hail the Cross,
    —*Our only hope.*

Third Station: Jesus Falls the First Time

We adore you, O Christ, and we praise you.
    —*Because by your holy Cross you have redeemed
    the world!*

A farmer plants grain in an act of sheer faith. As
each tiny kernel falls from coarse hands to the soil,
the farmer knows that grain is being lost to decay in
the dark earth but that this death is necessary for a
crop that yields thirty, sixty, or one hundredfold. A
single grain falls to the ground and does not remain
a single grain but provides bread in abundance.
    —*Jesus,
    you fell out of exhaustion, pain,
    and the sheer difficulty of your Way of the Cross.
    But your every step, your every fall, was not in
        vain.
    You offered your steps, your falls, and ultimately
        your whole life as a single grain of wheat that
        your Father might reap an abundant harvest in
        our lives.*

Lord Jesus, help us to see you in our every step and
stumble as we strive to be faithful to you.
Through your grace, may our failings yield a
bountiful harvest in our lives, our Church, and
our world.

Hail the Cross,
—*Our only hope.*

Fourth Station: Jesus Meets His Sorrowful Mother

We adore you, O Christ, and we praise you.
—*Because by your holy Cross you have redeemed*
the world!

A young man and young woman embrace their
mothers one last time before beginning a long
journey to an unknown future in a country far from
home. Knowing they may never see their mothers again, they are overcome with grief—unable to
go on. With quiet courage the women urge their
children to keep going, hoping they will escape the
poverty, war, and oppression that have taken the lives
of so many others. Bearing the searing pain of sepa-
ration, these mothers give their children the gift of
freedom to make the journey that lies before them.

—Jesus,
you met your mother's gaze and saw the pain she
was suffering.
Her presence and love gave you strength
to keep walking the road to Calvary.
Help us to look into the eyes of our sisters and
brothers throughout the world whose lives bear
the mystery of the Cross.
Amidst our own pain, open our hearts to see
the sorrows and burdens others bear.
Give us the courage and compassion to recognize
you in them and not look away.
In your mercy and through your gentle presence
give them and us comfort, and heal our sorrow.

Hail the Cross,
   —Our only hope.

Fifth Station: Simon Helps Jesus Carry the Cross

We adore you, O Christ, and we praise you.
   —Because by your holy Cross you have redeemed
   the world!

The laborer has many concerns to contend with:
the needs of his family, the pressures and long hours
of work, his personal worries and failings. As he
struggles to meet these competing responsibilities,

there is always someone who is asking for more.
What more can he give? What more does he have
to give? Yet each time he says yes; giving even more
of himself, he finds that he is somehow capable. He
knows the truth of receiving through giving.

—*Jesus,*
with Simon's help, you are not left alone to bear
your Cross.
Through the helping hands of our neighbors and
through your grace,
we also are not left alone to bear our crosses.
The strength of your grace is such
that even in the midst of our own struggles
we, like Simon, are able to stand with our
neighbors in their hour of need.
Grant us confidence in your help as we bear our
crosses, Lord Jesus,
that we may never despair in our hardships
nor shirk the opportunity to aid our neighbors.

Hail the Cross,
—*Our only hope.*

Sixth Station:
Veronica Wipes the Face of Jesus

We adore you, O Christ, and we praise you.
  —*Because by your holy Cross you have redeemed
  the world!*

His life had shone with hope and promise. His
friends were many, his grades were excellent, and his
prowess on the athletic field inspired cheers. Yet the
community gathered at his school one morning to
grieve his untimely death. All wanted to do and say
the right thing. So they offered prayers and remem-
bered stories. Yet only in wiping each other's tears
and sharing consoling embraces did they understand
that, although their hearts ached with sorrow, they
were not alone.

  —*Jesus,*
  you created quite a following.
  Many were excited about your ministry.
  Yet you were condemned to death
  and forced to carry your Cross through the
  crowded streets.
  Only a few offered comfort.
  Veronica did not remain with the crowd.
  She was bold enough to draw near to you and
  touch your face.

*She wiped the sweat and blood from your eyes and
    offered you comfort.*
*Lord Jesus, help us to have the strength and
    courage to touch the hurt of those who need us
    most.*

Hail the Cross,
  —*Our only hope.*

Seventh Station: Jesus Falls the Second Time

We adore you, O Christ, and we praise you.
  —*Because by your holy Cross you have redeemed
    the world!*

The missionaries gathered in the thatched-roof
hut of a forgotten village. A young mother was their
host. Halfway through dinner her husband arrived,
drunk and apologetic. In a town in which most
men leave to work elsewhere, he had stayed behind.
The following day they saw her again. It was Good
Friday. Kneeling down, she pressed her cheek against
the splintery wood of the Cross. She was crying.
When one falls, others are brought to their knees.
God's grace alone lifts us up.
  —*Jesus,
    you bore the Cross of the world's sinfulness.*

*That you fell shows the Cross was as heavy for you
    as it is for us.
That you continued onward speaks of your
    mission's triumphant power.
Let not the sins of others, nor the faults and
    failures of our own, be too great a burden for us.
May the grace that lifted and carried you be our
    strength.
And at the moment of trial, may your glory be our
    deepest desire.*

Hail the Cross,
    —*Our only hope.*

Eighth Station: Jesus Meets the Women
of Jerusalem

We adore you, O Christ, and we praise you.
    —*Because by your holy Cross you have redeemed
    the world!*

Though tired and exhausted from already having raised her own family, the woman wanted her
daughter to have a much better life than her own.
She would care for her new grandchild so that
her daughter could work and go to school. It was
enough for her to raise her own children, but to take
on that parental role again with her grandchildren is

something she never dreamed she would have to do.
Yet this grandmother's example continues to speak
the truth about love to her family.

> —*Jesus,*
> *in your words to the women on the way to the*
>   *Cross, you did not hide the truth.*
> *You spoke to them because they understood*
>   *what many of us often do not—*
> *a life sacrificed for love can bring new life.*
> *Prepare our hearts to listen as they did.*
> *Confide in us what you confided in them:*
>   *the mystery of sacrificial love.*
> *Teach us to understand what your suffering and*
>   *sacrifice have done for us,*
> *and assure us of the value that our sacrifices have*
>   *for others.*

Hail the Cross,
> —*Our only hope.*

Ninth Station: Jesus Falls the Third Time

We adore you, O Christ, and we praise you.
> —*Because by your holy Cross you have redeemed*
> *the world!*

An emaciated parent labors under a heavy burden. He knows not what weighs more, the load on

his shoulders or the weight of needing to guarantee his children's one meal for the day. In the scorching, unrelenting sun, and under the scornful stare of the unsympathetic multitude that elbows its hurried way, he trudges on, falling and rising, questioning the meaninglessness of his cursed life. Yet his efforts are not in vain, for he knows that, each time he falls and gets up again, he moves a little closer to ensuring a fleeting smile on the faces of his waiting children.

—Lord Jesus,
    your persistence, despite your battered and
      aching body, is a sure indicator of your steadfast
      commitment and steely resolve.
  Your desire to free us from the clutches of evil
      enabled you to rise after this last and most
      painful fall.
  Each move toward the peak of Mount Calvary
      was a step closer to achieving your mission.
  Help us not to be disheartened by the trying
      circumstances of our lives.
  Taking strength from your determination,
      may we get up and shoulder our crosses once
      more.

Hail the Cross,
  —*Our only hope.*

Tenth Station: Jesus Is Stripped
of His Garments

We adore you, O Christ, and we praise you.
   —*Because by your holy Cross you have redeemed
   the world!*

The soldiers began shouting and cursing at them
to take off all of their clothes and lay them in a
pile. A mother with her two small children watched
in anguish as her neighbors who refused or hesi-
tated were beaten and brutalized. When the soldiers
approached her, she slowly removed her clothes
while shaking with fear. She pulled her children
to her as she tried to cover their nakedness. This
humiliation was the last and final act of indignity
before they were herded to their deaths.
   —*Lord Jesus,*
   when they ripped away your tunic,
      opening anew the wounds where blood had
      dried to your clothing, they tried to wrench the
      last trace of dignity from you.
   You stood there naked for all to see and to mock,
      not knowing if the pain or the shame was
      harder to bear.
   You suffered indignity and humiliation at the
      hands of your tormentors

> *in order to restore to all of us the glorious dignity*
> *of the children of God.*
> *Teach us, Jesus, to recognize, respect, and cherish*
> *the precious dignity in each one of your children.*

Hail the Cross,
   —*Our only hope.*

Eleventh Station: Jesus Is Nailed to the Cross

We adore you, O Christ, and we praise you.
   —*Because by your holy Cross you have redeemed*
   the world!

A wayward soul, searching for meaning, enters the church and kneels. Like the Israelites—who looked to Moses' staff and bronze serpent for hope and healing—the searcher looks upon the image of the crucified. The image comforts, as if to say that life's present sufferings are not in vain. It mysteriously and eternally points to a God who heals, redeems, and brings life in the midst of death. In the Cross, we find not only life but hope in life eternal.

   —*Jesus,*
   the physical torment you endured was
   excruciating, but perhaps more painful for you
   was having to see
   the anguished face of your mother.

> *In that moment, you united your hearts in love*
>   *and sorrow as you offered your mutual*
>   *sufferings for our redemption.*
> *Lord Jesus, when swords of suffering and loneliness*
>   *pierce our hearts, may we have the eyes of faith*
>   *to see you and your mother gazing upon us*
>   *compassionately.*
> *Unite your Sacred Heart and her sorrowful Heart*
>   *with ours.*
> *Help us embrace the crosses we bear*
>   *with your response of love and acceptance.*

Hail the Cross,
   —*Our only hope.*

Twelfth Station: Jesus Dies on the Cross

We adore you, O Christ, and we praise you.
   —*Because by your holy Cross you have redeemed
   the world!*

The elderly priest raises the host, then the cup:
"This is my Body. . . . This is the Chalice of my Blood.
. . . Do this in memory of me." Even after repeating
these sacred actions thousands of times, he remains
in awe of the mystery they recall and once again
make real—Christ's sacrifice on the Cross. This is the
same sacrifice the elderly priest has sought to imitate

for his flock. As he distributes Holy Communion
with the words "Body of Christ," "Blood of Christ,"
he declares what each person receives and what each
becomes: the presence of Christ as food for the
world.

—*Lord Jesus,*
by your suffering and death on the Cross,
you brought life to the world.
Each time we receive Holy Communion,
we are immersed in your death and resurrection.
Your gift of love, offered freely on the Cross,
becomes for us now the food of our salvation.
Help us to live in faithful response to so great a
sacrifice.
Help us die to self so that we may live for others.

Hail the Cross,
—*Our only hope.*

Thirteenth Station: Jesus Is Taken Down from the Cross

We adore you, O Christ, and we praise you.
—*Because by your holy Cross you have redeemed*
the world!

Holding her dying child, the young mother
silently screams her questions to God: Why my

child? Why this innocent suffering? Why now? She feels the warmth ebb away as death takes its final toll. She wonders why her heart continues to beat while her child's is now silent. She closes her eyes and painfully sees the long struggle ahead of her—begging for a little more time, holding on, fearing to let go, and struggling to set her child free.

   —*Jesus,*
   your lifeless body now rests in the arms of your
     sorrowful mother.
   As she received you into her womb at Nazareth,
     held you at Bethlehem, clung to you on the flight
     into Egypt, reached out to you in the Temple at
     Jerusalem, and walked with you to Calvary,
     her arms now cling to you while her tears cleanse
     your crucified body.
   Lord Jesus, your mother's pierced heart
     opened her arms to hold the suffering of our
     world.
   Pierce our hearts with your grace and open our
     arms to others.
   Make us the bearers of your comfort
     and your healing in our bruised and broken
     world.

Hail the Cross,
   —*Our only hope.*

Fourteenth Station: Jesus Is Laid in the Tomb

We adore you, O Christ, and we praise you.
—*Because by your holy Cross you have redeemed*
the world!

In the dark of night, the mourners gather silently around the open grave. The circumstances surrounding the death do not permit a daytime burial. A small oil lamp provides the only light for the men as they jump down into the hole to lower the simple coffin. As the body of their loved one disappears into the shadows of the grave, the mourners' anguished cries pierce the stillness of the night. The distinctive thump of dirt hitting the wood of casket deepens their sense of loss.

—*Lord Jesus,*
by humbling yourself and being faithful to the
point of death,
you entered into the deepest darkness of our world,
the darkness of death.
Grant us the eyes of faith so as not to lose sight of
you in the face of death.
May the light of your life, the light that conquers
all, pierce and dispel the darkness of death.
Reveal to us the journey from this world into life
eternal with you.

Hail the Cross,
  —*Our only hope.*

Closing Prayer

Lord Jesus,
your Cross is our only hope.
The love that compelled you to take the steps to
    Calvary
is the very love that conquered sin and death
    forever
through your glorious resurrection.
Each time we follow the way of your passion,
we learn again that you redeem our steps, pick us
    up from our falls,
and unite our sacrifices and sufferings with yours
in the transforming power of your Cross.
Led and redeemed by you, our Savior,
may we die only to rise with you in glory.

We adore you, O Christ, and we praise you.
  —*Because by your holy Cross you have redeemed
  the world!*

May almighty God bless us and keep us:
the Father, the Son, and the Holy Spirit.
Amen.

✣ VI ✣
Prayers

GOD HAS breathed his very breath into us. We speak to God with the yearning and the words of sons to a Father because the Spirit has made us adopted children in Christ. The same Spirit who provides us with the energy and impetus to follow after the Lord and to accept His mission also give us the desire and the utterance for prayer.

Our thoughts are not easily God's thoughts, nor our wills His will. But as we listen to Him and converse with Him, our minds will be given to understand Him and His designs. The more we come through prayer to relish what is right, the better we shall work in our mission for the realization of the kingdom. (*Constitution 3:21–22*)

Prayers for Holy Cross

---

48. WEEKLY PRAYERS FOR VOCATIONS TO THE CONGREGATION OF HOLY CROSS

---

*These prayers may be used individually or communally;
if said by one person only, all parts are prayed by the
individual.*

Sunday: The Eucharist

Lord God, you instilled in the heart of Basil
Moreau a fervent devotion to the presence of your
Son in the Eucharist.
—*Fill our hearts with gratitude for the "excesses
of God's tenderness" made present to us in the
Eucharistic mystery.*

Draw the hearts of your people into loving communion with the heart of your Son, and call young
people to offer their lives in the service of others as
Holy Cross religious. We ask this through Christ our
Lord. Amen.

Monday: Zeal

Lord God, you filled the heart of Basil Moreau with zeal for the proclamation of your kingdom.
—*Fortify our hearts with the gift of zeal,
the "burning desire to make God known, loved,
and served."*

Enkindle in the hearts of all believers zeal for your kingdom, and inspire young people to become disciples eager to serve as educators in the faith in the Family of Holy Cross. We ask this through Christ our Lord. Amen.

Tuesday: Divine Providence

Lord God, you enlivened the heart of Basil Moreau with a profound trust in your Divine Providence.
—*Fill our hearts with a deep conviction of your
loving care, and help us to know that "Holy Cross
is not a human work, but God's very own."*

Show forth your providential love in the lives of all, and draw into your service new members of the Family of Holy Cross. We ask this through Christ our Lord. Amen.

Wednesday: Unity

Lord God, you filled the heart of Basil Moreau with a passion for the unity of Holy Cross modeled on the mystery of the Holy Family.
—*Pour forth in our hearts a yearning for such "conformity of sentiments, interests, and wills as to make all of us one . . . as the Father, Son, and Holy Spirit are one."*

Grace your faithful people with a share in your own divine life, and call young people to join their lives with ours in the Family of Holy Cross. We ask this through Christ our Lord. Amen.

Thursday: Conformity to Christ

Lord God, you infused the heart of Basil Moreau with a yearning "to imitate the conduct of Jesus Christ."
—*Penetrate our hearts with a longing "to so well assimilate the thoughts, judgments, desires, words, and actions of Jesus Christ that we can say with the great Apostle: 'I no longer live, it is Christ who lives in me.'"*

Pour forth your Spirit into your community that our lives will conform more deeply to the Sacred Heart of your Son, and bring to Holy Cross those

who long to imitate his love. We ask this through
Christ our Lord. Amen.

Friday: The Cross

Lord God, you formed in the heart of Basil
Moreau the capacity to embrace the Cross, "a treasure more valuable than gold and precious stones."
—Fill our hearts that we may see our suffering
and that of others as relics of the sacred wood of the
true Cross which we must love and venerate.

Lord, may we be grateful for the gift of redemp-
tion revealed in the Cross. Summon to life in Holy
Cross young people who desire to proclaim with us,
Hail, O Cross, our only hope. We ask this through
Christ our Lord. Amen.

Saturday: Our Lady of Sorrows

Lord God, you graced the heart of Basil Moreau
with the desire to entrust his religious family to Our
Lady of Holy Cross, the Mother of Sorrows.
—Open our hearts to the tender love
that comes to us through the mother of Jesus,
who stood at the foot of the Cross when Jesus offered
himself to the Father for our salvation.

Fill the hearts of your people with the compassion of your Sorrowful Mother, and through her intercession draw to life in Holy Cross young people who desire to care for others. We ask this through Christ our Lord. Amen.

49. FOR VOCATIONS

Holy Mary, Our Lady of Holy Cross,
your Son instructed his disciples to pray
that the Lord of the harvest supply workers for the
    kingdom.
Faithful to Jesus' instruction we come to you, our
    mother and patroness,
and beg you to intercede with your Son for an
    increase of vocations to religious life in the
    Family of Holy Cross.
Confident that Holy Cross is not a human work
but God's very own,
and that Divine Providence has inspired and
    sustained our life in Holy Cross,
we entrust our future to your maternal care.

As a woman of sorrow,
whose heart was filled with compassion for those
    who suffer,

pray that men and women of compassion will
    accept God's call
to make God known, loved, and served
through their life and ministry in the Family of
    Holy Cross.
Amen.

---

50. FOR THE CONGREGATION OF HOLY CROSS

God our Father,
we thank you for having called us to Holy Cross,
to live and work together for the mission of Christ.
Transform our minds and hearts,
and guide us along the pathways of truth.

Lord Jesus,
let us experience the peace and joy
of your presence in our midst.
Make us faithful disciples,
educators in the faith,
servants who are sensitive to the poor and needy.

Holy Spirit of God,
enlighten and strengthen us
in living and proclaiming the good news of
    salvation,

so that the witness of our religious life
may be a sign of hope in the Church and in our
    world.

Hear this prayer,
Father, Son, and Holy Spirit,
one God, forever and ever.
Amen.

✢ ✢ ✢ ✢ ✢ ✢ ✢ ✢

*By zeal is understood that flame of burning desire which
one feels to make God known, loved, and served and thus
save souls.*

—**Blessed Basil Moreau** (*Christian
Pedagogy* I:1, art. 4)

✢ ✢ ✢ ✢ ✢ ✢ ✢ ✢

51. For the Family of Holy Cross (I)

Almighty God,
source of light and glory,
through the Gospel of Jesus Christ and the Family
    of Holy Cross

you have called us to make your truth and justice
  known.

Like the stars in the heavens,
may we extend your light throughout the world,
a world enslaved by injustice and war,
hatred, mistrust, and division.

May our example and teaching
be a means to transform minds and hearts,
to prepare the world for better times,
for the coming of your reign.

Empower us with hope in your glory,
so we can remain faithful
and complete the work you have entrusted to us.
We ask this through Christ Jesus our Lord.
Amen.

52. For the Family of Holy Cross (II)

Provident God,
you inspired Basil Moreau
to form a family of three societies,
men and women, lay and ordained,
to be a sign of love and unity in a world of division.

May we, as brothers, sisters, and priests of Holy Cross,
be more closely joined in our bond of mutual charity
and in fidelity to our vows,
for in unity is our strength.

We pray that our witness of mutual respect and
   shared undertaking
will be a hopeful sign of the kingdom,
where others can behold how we love one another.

Bless and strengthen our collaborative efforts, our
   shared mission,
and our communion of vocation,
that like a mighty tree
Holy Cross will grow and spring forth
new limbs and branches around the world,
bringing hope, justice, and love to those in need.
We pray this through Jesus Christ our Lord and
   brother.
Amen.

53. For the Family of Holy Cross (III)

Lord God,
you inspired our founder, Basil Moreau,
to establish the religious Family of Holy Cross

and to call us to live and work together
as "a visible imitation of the Holy Family."
The common life and work of Holy Cross
was to be "a powerful lever with which to move,
direct, and sanctify the world."
Enable in your Family of Holy Cross
a deeper fidelity to the founding vision of Basil
  Moreau so we might be a sign of God's love
and tender mercy to people everywhere.
We ask this through Christ our Lord.
Amen.

54. FOR HOLY CROSS COLLABORATORS AND ASSOCIATES

Gracious God,
we ask your blessing on those men and women
who share in the mission of Holy Cross
through their prayer and dedicated work in our
  ministries.
In their collaboration with us,
may they not only recognize and develop their own
  gifts,
but also discover the deepest longing in their lives.
Increase their commitment to the mission,
their zeal for ministry,

and their devotion to our beloved founder, Basil
   Moreau.
Bless their families and loved ones,
and may they truly be men and women
with hope to bring.
We make our prayer through Jesus Christ your Son,
with Mary, our Sorrowful Mother, at our side.
Amen.

---

55. For Those to Whom We Minister

Loving Father,
as we come as servant and neighbor
to support men and women of goodwill
in their efforts to form communities of the coming
   kingdom,
clasp us more firmly to yourself
and use our hands and minds
to do the work only you can do.
Bless all those you have entrusted to our ministry.
Help them to recognize and discover their own gifts
and to place them at the service of your kingdom.
Help them to discover the deepest longing in their
   lives
and to know you alone as their fulfillment.
Help them to experience at each and every moment

the depth of your love in the gift of your Son and
    Spirit,
so that they may have life and have it abundantly!
Amen.

---

56. FOR PERSEVERANCE IN RELIGIOUS LIFE

Gracious God,
in the mystery of your wisdom you have called me
to religious life in the Congregation of Holy Cross.
By my prayerful observance
of chastity, poverty, and obedience,
may my life call into question
the fascinations of our world:
pleasure, wealth, and power.
Give me, Lord,
the grace of joy, integrity, and perseverance
in my holy vocation,
so that I may serve you faithfully
until the end of my days.
I make this prayer through Christ, my Lord and
    brother.
Amen.

✢ ✢ ✢ ✢ ✢ ✢ ✢

*To become a worthy religious of Holy Cross, you must
cultivate an habitual union of heart with God. . . .
You must be accustomed to a great union of heart with
God now; this union cannot be attained without an
increasing fidelity to prayer.*

—Blessed Basil Moreau (*Exercises of 1855*)

✢ ✢ ✢ ✢ ✢ ✢ ✢

57. FOR PERSONAL RENEWAL OF VOWS

Eternal God, loving Father,
mindful of your call
to share in the mission of Christ, your Son,
I affirm my commitment
to the apostolic religious life.
I wish to continue living the Gospel in this way
and so renew before you today
my vows of chastity, poverty, and obedience
according to the Constitutions
of the Congregation of Holy Cross.
Believing in the presence of the Spirit in my life,
I rely upon your grace to strengthen my resolve
to be ever faithful to this commitment.
Amen.

58. FOR A SPIRIT OF OBEDIENCE

(from the Spiritual Exercises for the Marianites of Holy Cross by Father Moreau)

You are my Lord and my God!
Command—here I am ready to do anything to
    obey you!
Call, and I will answer;
inspire, and I will act;
reveal your divine will to me,
and I will do it, all for love,
because you are a God of love
and by love you reign in faithful hearts
and exercise your powerful dominion here.

59. FOR THOSE IN AUTHORITY IN THE CONGREGATION

God of wisdom,
be with our brothers who have responded to your call
to leadership in the Congregation of Holy Cross.
Strengthen them to preach and witness to the Gospel.
Give them words that challenge us
to be responsible for the common good;
Give them vision and perception

to read the signs of our times;
Give them hearts of compassion
to care for the well-being of each person.
God of truth,
stir in them the same passion
that impelled Basil Moreau
to respond to the needs of his time.
May his spirit inspire them
with the competence to see and the courage to act.
Protect them from weariness and discouragement.
Bless them with the sure knowledge
of your presence and providence, now and always.
We ask this in the name of Jesus the Lord.
Amen.

60. For Our Benefactors

Gracious God,
pour out your blessings on our benefactors.
Their goodness has encouraged us,
and their gifts have enhanced our mission
to be educators in the faith,
supporting men and women of grace and goodwill
    everywhere
in our efforts to form communities of the coming
    kingdom.

In gratitude, we ask you
to reward them with signs of your generous love
and, when their lives here on earth have ended,
to welcome them to your heavenly banquet,
through Jesus Christ our Lord.
Amen.

✣ ✣ ✣ ✣ ✣ ✣ ✣ ✣

Prayers for a Dying Religious

Father Moreau encouraged his religious to meditate regularly on their death so that they might more readily abandon their attachments to relationships, possessions, and the esteem of others. Meditation on death can assist religious in the effort to discipline the body, which returns to dust, in order to prepare the whole person for judgment before God. Such meditation can lead to contrition and to greater frequency of the sacrament of Reconciliation and Communion. Father Moreau encouraged his religious to pray to Saint Joseph for a happy death. (See section VII, Saint Joseph.)

61. LITANY FOR A DYING RELIGIOUS

(adapted from the 1947 Directory and Pastoral Care of the Sick, 1983)

It would be appropriate at some point to add the patron saints of the dying religious.

Lord, have mercy	Lord, have mercy
Christ, have mercy	Christ, have mercy
Lord, have mercy	Lord, have mercy

Holy Mary, Mother of God	pray for him
All you holy Angels and Archangels	pray for him
Holy Abel	pray for him
All you choirs of the just	pray for him
Holy Abraham	pray for him
Saint John the Baptist	pray for him
Saint Joseph	pray for him
All you holy Patriarchs and Prophets	pray for him
Saint Peter	pray for him
Saint Paul	pray for him
Saint Andrew	pray for him
Saint John	pray for him
All you holy Apostles and Evangelists	pray for him
All you holy disciples of Our Lord	pray for him
All you Holy Innocents	pray for him
Saint Stephen	pray for him

Saint Lawrence	pray for him
All you holy martyrs	pray for him
Saint Sylvester	pray for him
Saint Gregory	pray for him
Saint Augustine	pray for him
All you holy bishops and confessors	pray for him
Saint Benedict	pray for him
Saint Francis	pray for him
All you holy monks and hermits	pray for him
Saint Mary Magdalene	pray for him
Saint Lucy	pray for him
All you holy virgins and widows	pray for him
Saint André Bessette	pray for him
Blessed Basil Moreau	pray for him
Blessed Marie-Léonie Paradis	pray for him
All holy men and women	pray for him
Lord, be merciful	Lord, save our brother
From all evil	Lord, save our brother
From every sin	Lord, save our brother
From Satan's power	Lord, save our brother
At the moment of death	Lord, save our brother
From everlasting death	Lord, save our brother
On the day of judgment	Lord, save our brother
By your coming as man	Lord, save our brother
By your suffering and Cross	Lord, save our brother
By your death and rising to new life	Lord, save our brother
By your return in glory to the Father	Lord, save our brother
By your gift of the Holy Spirit	Lord, save our brother

By your coming again in glory	Lord, save our brother
Be merciful to us sinners	Lord, hear our prayer
Bring N. to eternal life, first promised to him in baptism	Lord, hear our prayer
Raise N. on the last day for he has eaten the bread of life	Lord, hear our prayer
Let N. share in your glory, for he has shared in your suffering and death	Lord, hear our prayer
Jesus, Son of the living God	Lord, hear our prayer
Christ, hear us	Christ, hear us
Lord Jesus, hear our prayer	Lord Jesus, hear our prayer

Let us pray.

Remember not, O Lord,
the sins of our brother, N.,
but, according to your great mercy,
be mindful of him in your eternal glory.
Let the heavens be opened to him,
and let the angels rejoice with him.
May Saint Michael, the Archangel, the chief of the
heavenly host, conduct him;
may blessed Peter, the Apostle, to whom were given
the keys of the kingdom of heaven, receive him;
may holy Paul, the Apostle, and chosen vessel of
election, assist him;
and may Saint John, the beloved disciple,

to whom the secrets of heaven were revealed,
    intercede for him;
may all the holy Apostles, to whom was given
the power of binding and loosing, pray for him;
may all the chosen servants and blessed martyrs of God,
who, in this world, have suffered torments for the
    sake of Christ,
intercede for him,
that being delivered from this body of corruption,
he may be admitted into the kingdom of heaven.
Through the assistance and merits of our Lord
    Jesus Christ,
who lives and reigns with the Father and the Holy Spirit,
world without end.
Amen.

---

62. Prayer by a Dying Religious

(adapted from the 1947 Directory)

Give me grace, O God,
to accept this time of death,
and give me the dispositions and strength
to perfectly accomplish your will.
Sanctify death for me
through the merits of the death of your Son;
may his divine words uttered on the Cross,

"Father, forgive them,"
obtain from your goodness
the remission of my sins.
May the burning thirst which Jesus had
for your glory and my salvation
enkindle in my heart
an ardent desire to glorify you.
May the words spoken by him
when at the moment of death
he recommended his soul to you
lead you to receive my soul
at the hour of my death.
May the words pronounced by Jesus,
"It is finished,"
obtain for me the grace that, before I die,
you may bring to completion in me
all the honor and glory which are your due.
May the sacred water which flowed from his side
wash away my sins,
and may his heart, which was pierced for me,
serve as my place of refuge.
Conceal me in your tabernacle,
which is the loving heart of your Son, my Savior;
shelter me from the snares of my enemies
in that divine sanctuary and in his sacred wounds.
Remember, O my God,
it is you who brought me forth from my mother's womb,
and preserve me in this world,

and who will never abandon me.
Holy Mary, Mother of God,
patroness of our Congregation,
pray for me, a poor sinner,
at this, my hour of death.
Saint Joseph,
protector and patron of the Congregation
in which I have the grace to die,
be my intercessor and advocate with God
and be pleased to give me your protection
at this, my hour of death.
Amen.

63. PRAYER OF COMMENDATION

Go forth, Christian soul, from this world
in the name of God the almighty Father,
who created you,
in the name of Jesus Christ,
Son of the living God,
who suffered for you,
in the name of the Holy Spirit,
who was poured out upon you;
go forth, Christian soul.
May you live in peace this day;
may your home be with God in Zion,

with Mary, the virgin Mother of God,
with Joseph, and all the angels and saints.

✠ ✠ ✠ ✠ ✠ ✠ ✠ ✠

*You know, it is permitted to desire death if one's unique
goal is to go toward God. When I die, I will go to heaven
and I will be much closer to God than I am now. I will
have more power to help you.*

—**Saint André Bessette**

✠ ✠ ✠ ✠ ✠ ✠ ✠ ✠

64. PRAYER AFTER DEATH (I)

Almighty and eternal God,
hear our prayers for your son, our brother N.,
whom you have called from this life to yourself.
Grant him light, happiness, and peace.
Let him pass in safety through the gates of death,
and live forever with all your saints
in the light you promised to Abraham
and to all his descendants in faith.
Guard him from all harm,
and on that great day of resurrection and reward
raise him up with all your saints.

Pardon his sins
and give him eternal reward in your kingdom.
We ask this through Christ, our Lord.
Amen.

65. Prayer after Death (II)

Loving and merciful God,
we entrust our brother to your mercy.
You loved him greatly in this life;
now that he is freed from all its cares,
give him happiness and peace forever.
The old order has passed away;
welcome him now into paradise
where there will be no more sorrow,
no more weeping or pain,
but only peace and joy
with Jesus, your Son,
and the Holy Spirit
forever and ever.
Amen.

✠ ✠ ✠ ✠ ✠ ✠ ✠

Intercessory Prayers and Prayers for Individual Canonizations

66. FOR THE INTERCESSION OF BLESSED BASIL MOREAU AND SAINT ANDRÉ BESSETTE

In many communities, the prayers invoking Blessed Basil Moreau and Saint André Bessette are prayed daily at the conclusion of the intercessions for Morning Prayer. (See below, no. I under Blessed Basil Moreau and no. I under Saint André Bessette.)

Blessed Basil Moreau

I

Lord God,
through the intercession of Blessed Basil Moreau,
help us to imitate his virtues,
> —*Especially his trust in Divine Providence,
> his confidence in the Cross as our only hope,
> and his zeal for the apostolate.*

II

Lord Jesus,
source of all that is good,
you inspired Basil Moreau
to found the religious Family of Holy Cross
to continue your mission among the People of God.
May he be for us a model of apostolic life,
an example of fidelity,
and an inspiration as we strive to follow you.

Lord Jesus,
you said, "Ask and you shall receive."
We come to ask you that you hear our prayer.
It is through the intercession of Basil Moreau that
    we ask . . . .

May we learn to imitate his holiness and service
and look to him confidently in times of need.
Amen.

✢ ✢ ✢ ✢ ✢ ✢ ✢ ✢

The most efficacious means of strengthening ourselves in virtue and rooting us in the land of the saints where we have been planted . . . is to implore often help from on high and above all to listen to that interior voice which speaks to us in meditation.

—**Blessed Basil Moreau** (*Exercises of 1858*)

✢ ✢ ✢ ✢ ✢ ✢ ✢ ✢

Saint André Bessette

I

Through the prayers and example
of Saint André Bessette,
　—*May we grow in our devotion to Saint Joseph,
　and in our commitment to the poor and the
　afflicted.*

II

Lord,
you have chosen Brother André to spread devotion
　to Saint Joseph
and to dedicate himself to all those who are poor
　and afflicted.
Grant through his intercession
the favor that we now request . . . .
Grant us the grace to imitate his piety and charity

so that, with him, we may share the reward
promised to all who care for their neighbors
out of love for you.
We make this prayer in the name of Jesus the Lord.

✣ ✣ ✣ ✣ ✣ ✣ ✣ ✣ ✣

*It is with the smallest brushes that the artist paints the
most exquisitely beautiful pictures.*

—Saint André Bessette

✣ ✣ ✣ ✣ ✣ ✣ ✣ ✣ ✣

67. FOR THE CANONIZATION OF OUR SERVANTS OF GOD

*The following intercession may be inserted before the
necrology and final intercession for the deceased at Vespers.*

Lord God,
grant that the Church may recognize
those Holy Cross religious
who are Servants of God:
[Patrick Peyton, Theotonius Ganguly,
Vincent McCauley, and Flavien Laplante,]
    —*Especially in their veneration*

of the Blessed Virgin Mary,
their missionary zeal,
and their service of others.

68. ADDITIONAL PRAYERS FOR INDIVIDUAL CANONIZATIONS

Blessed Basil Moreau

O God,
you are most admirable in your saints.
We ask you to grant
that the Church may glorify,
at the earliest opportunity,
Blessed Basil Moreau,
Founder of the Congregation of Holy Cross.
May we be led to imitate his virtues.

We ask this through Christ our Lord.
Amen.

Blessed Marie-Léonie Paradis

Good and gracious God,
you Son willed to live in the home of Mary and Joseph,
obedient to the law of life in our world.
We ask you to grant

that the Church may glorify,
at the earliest opportunity,
Blessed Marie-Léonie Paradis,
Foundress of the Little Sisters of the Holy Family.

We ask this through Christ our Lord.
Amen.

Servant of God Patrick Peyton

Lord God,
Father Peyton devoted his priestly life
to strengthening the families of the world
by calling them to pray together every day,
  especially the Rosary.
We ask you, therefore,
to hasten the day of his canonization
so that your faithful people everywhere
who remember his message,
that "the family that prays together stays together,"
will imitate him in his devotion
to the Mother of your Son,
and will be inspired by his holy life
to draw ever closer to you
with childlike confidence and love.

We ask this through Christ our Lord.
Amen.

Servant of God Theotonius Amal Ganguly

Gracious God,
we thank you for the gift of your servant,
Archbishop Theotonius Ganguly,
to the Church and to the people of Bangladesh.
By his goodness, gentleness, and kindness,
you guided your people through times of suffering,
     deprivation, and war.
We pray that you may glorify without delay
him who consecrated to your glory and service
his life of labor and sacrifice.

We ask this in the name of Jesus the Lord.
Amen.

Servant of God Vincent Joseph McCauley

God, our loving Father,
we thank you for the gift of your servant,
Bishop Vincent McCauley,
to the Church and to the people of East Africa,
and in particular to the diocese of Fort Portal.
By his goodness, gentleness, kindness, and
     innovation,
you guided your people
through times of ignorance, poverty, and suffering.
His endurance of physical pain,

and his example of humility, self-giving,
deep faith, and pastoral zeal,
were an inspiration to many people.
We pray that you may glorify without delay
him who consecrated to your glory and service
his life of labor and sacrifice.

We ask this through Christ our Lord.
Amen.

Servant of God Flavien Laplante

Lord God,
we give you joyful thanks
for the life of Brother Flavien Laplante,
hermit and apostle to the fishermen of Diang.
Through his prayers, his apostolic courage,
and his concern for others,
he restored dignity to neglected people in
    Bangladesh
and provided for the care of orphans.
His devotion to Mary, his enthusiasm,
and his humble life of generous service to the poor
    and needy
invite us to dedicate ourselves to you
by a life of service to those in need.
We ask you, therefore, to hasten the day
of his canonization for the good of all people,

especially for the Church and the people of
Bangladesh.

Grant this through Christ our Lord.
Amen.

Jacques-François Dujarié

(1947 Directory)

Almighty and eternal God,
who inspired your servant, Jacques-François
Dujarié,
to found the Brothers of Saint Joseph
and the Sisters of Providence of Ruillé
for the good of souls,
we beseech you to glorify without delay
him who consecrated to your glory and service
his life of labor and sacrifice.

We ask this through Jesus Christ our Lord.
Amen.

69. For a Favor through the Intercession of:

Blessed Marie-Léonie Paradis

O God,
you are admirable in all your saints.
we ask you to grant us,
through the intercession of Mother Marie-Léonie,
the faithful servant of the Holy Family,
the favor of . . .
May she be glorified
and may we imitate her virtues.

We ask this through Jesus Christ our Lord.
Amen.

Servants of God Patrick Peyton, Theotonius Ganguly, or Vincent McCauley

Lord,
we ask that you bring many to know and imitate
the virtues of your Servant, N.,
and to benefit by his devotion to you
and to the service of others.
We ask you through his intercession

to grant us the favor of . . .
May his life inspire us to follow his example,
and may the recognition of his virtues
bring honor to the Church and glory to your
    name.
Amen.

Servant of God Flavien Laplante

Lord Jesus,
you said, "Ask and you shall receive."
We come to you to ask that you hear our prayer.
It is through the intercession of Brother Flavien
    Laplante that we ask . . .
May Brother Flavien's example
encourage us to carry our own cross with patience
and to strive to imitate his virtues
in our daily life of service to others.

We ask this grace of you
who live and reign
in union with the Father and the Holy Spirit,
now and forever.
Amen.

Jacques-François Dujarié

Almighty God,
you share your loving presence
with your saints in glory.
I ask you through the intercession
of your servant, Jacques-François Dujarié,
to grant me the favor I ask . . .
May we be inspired to imitate
his life and apostolic commitment,
through Jesus Christ our Lord.
Amen.

✣ ✣ ✣ ✣ ✣ ✣ ✣ ✣

We should bow down before the invisible hand of
Providence which directs all the events of this world for
God's greater glory and the salvation of the elect.
—Blessed Basil Moreau (*Circular Letter 47*)

✣ ✣ ✣ ✣ ✣ ✣ ✣ ✣

✜ ✜ ✜ ✜ ✜ ✜ ✜ ✜

Other Prayers

---

70. FOR THE POPE (I)

Let us pray for our Holy Father, Pope N.
   —*May the Lord preserve him,*
   give him a long life,
   make him blessed upon the earth,
   and may the Lord not hand him over
   to the power of his enemies.

May your hand be upon your holy servant.
   —*Upon your son whom you have chosen for this*
   ministry.

Let us pray.
O God,
the pastor and ruler of all the faithful,
in your mercy look upon your servant, N.,
whom you have appointed to preside over your
   Church.
Grant, we beseech you,

that by word and example
he may edify all those under his charge
so that, with the flock entrusted to him,
he may arrive at length unto life everlasting.
We ask this through Christ our Lord.
Amen.

71. FOR THE POPE (II)
(from the Roman Missal)

O God,
who in your providential design
willed that your Church
be built upon blessed Peter,
whom you set over the other apostles,
look with favor, we pray, on N. our Pope,
and grant that he whom you have made Peter's successor
may be for your people a visible source and foundation
of unity in faith and communion.
Through our Lord Jesus Christ, your Son,
who lives and reigns with you in the unity of the
    Holy Spirit,
one God, for ever and ever.
Amen.

72. FOR THE LOCAL CHURCH

(from the Roman Missal)

O God,
who in each pilgrim Church throughout the world
make visible the one, holy, catholic, and apostolic Church,
graciously grant
that your faithful people of this diocese of N.
may be so united to their shepherd
and gathered together in the Holy Spirit
through the Gospel and the Eucharist,
as to worthily embody the universality of your people
and become a sign and instrument in the world
of the presence of Christ.
Who lives and reigns with you in the unity of the
    Holy Spirit,
one God, for ever and ever.
Amen.

73. FOR THE DIOCESAN BISHOP

(from the Roman Missal)

O God,
shepherd and ruler of all the faithful,
look favorably on your servant N.,

whom you have set at the head
of your Church of N. as her shepherd;
grant, we pray, that by word and example
he may be of service to those over whom he presides,
so that, together with the flock entrusted to his care,
he may come to everlasting life.
Through our Lord Jesus Christ, your Son,
who lives and reigns with you in the unity of the
    Holy Spirit,
one God, for ever and ever.
Amen.

---

74. FOR GOVERNMENT AND WORLD LEADERS
(based on 1988 Constitutions)

Lord God,
on the night before he died for us
Jesus, your Son, washed the feet of his disciples
and proclaimed that he came into the world
not to be served but to serve.
Inspire all government and world leaders
with Jesus' vision of authority.
Enable in them a preferential love for the poor and
    the afflicted.
Grant them the competence to see.

and the courage to act in accord with the common good
Fill them with a passion for justice
and speed their steps along the way of peace,
so that every people and nation will taste on earth
some share of the fullness of your reign of justice,
      love, and peace.

We make this prayer in the name of Jesus the Lord.
Amen.

---

75. *Veni, Creator Spiritus*
(Rabanus Maurus [776–856])

Veni, Creator Spiritus,
mentes tuorum visita,
imple superna gratia
quæ tu creasti pectora.

Qui diceris Paraclitus,
altissimi donum Dei,
fons vivus, ignis, caritas,
et spiritalis unctio.

Tu, septiformis munere,
digitus paternæ dexteræ,
tu rite promissum Patris,
sermone ditans guttura.

Accende lumen sensibus:
infunde amorem cordibus.
infirma nostri corporis
virtute firmans perpeti.

Hostem repella longius,
pacemque dones protinus:
ductore sic te prævio
vitemus omne noxium.

Per te sciamus da Patrem,
noscamus atque Filium;
Teque utriusque Spiritum
Credamus omni tempore.

Deo Patri sit gloria,
et Filio, qui a mortuis
surrexit, ac Paraclito,
in sæculorum sæcula. Amen.

Most Holy Spirit come this day
And fill the hearts which you have made;
With your abundant gifts of grace
Increase your presence in our souls.

For you are called our Advocate,
Consoling Gift from God Most High,
True living Fount and Fire of Love,
Eternal Source of happiness.

You lavish graces sevenfold,
Like finger of Right Hand divine;
You are the Father's promised Gift
To help us witness to the truth.

Instill your light into our minds
And flood our hearts with joy and love;
And with your strength which cannot fail,
Repair the weakness of our state.

Our deadly foe keep far away,
Bestow on us your wondrous peace;
Be with us ev'rywhere we go
To guard us from all sin and harm.

May we the Father know through you
And grow in knowledge of the Son,
And love you, Spirit of them both
In time and in eternity. Amen.

76. FOR THE INVOCATION OF THE SEVEN GIFTS OF THE HOLY SPIRIT

(Saint Bonaventure)

Lord Jesus,
as God's Spirit came down and rested upon you,
may the same Spirit rest upon us,
bestowing his sevenfold gifts.

Grant us the gift of *understanding*,
by which your precepts may enlighten our minds.
Grant us *counsel*,
by which we may follow in your footsteps
on the path of righteousness.
Grant us *courage*,
by which we may ward off the Enemy's attacks.
Grant us *knowledge*,
by which we can distinguish good from evil.
Grant us *piety*,
by which we may acquire compassionate hearts.
Grant us *fear*,
by which we may draw back from evil and submit
   to what is good.
Lastly, grant us *wisdom*,
that we may taste fully the life-giving sweetness of
   your love.
You live and reign forever and ever.
Amen.

✠ ✠ ✠ ✠ ✠ ✠ ✠

God gave us the commandments and it is in observing
them that we show whether we love God. Pray that you
may obtain a true love of God. God loves us so much. He
wants us to love him.

—Saint André Bessette

✠ ✠ ✠ ✠ ✠ ✠ ✠

77. TO THE HOLY SPIRIT

O God, all hearts are open to you, and every wish
    and secret is known.
Cleanse our thoughts by the inpouring of the Holy Spirit,
and grant us the grace to love you perfectly and
    praise you worthily.
May the holy Comforter, who proceeds from you,
    O Lord,
enlighten our minds and teach us all truth as your
    Son has promised.

O Lord, let the power of the Holy Spirit be with us,
gently cleansing our hearts and guarding us against
    danger.

O God, you have instructed the hearts of the faithful
by the light of the Holy Spirit.

Grant that through the same Holy Spirit we may be
    truly wise
and rejoice in his consolation.
Amen.

78. For Spiritual Discernment
(Saint Benedict)

Gracious and holy Father,
please give me intellect to understand you,
reason to discern you,
diligence to seek you,
wisdom to find you,
a spirit to know you,
a heart to meditate upon you,
ears to hear you,
eyes to see you,
a tongue to proclaim you,
a way of life pleasing to you,
patience to wait for you,
and perseverance to look for you.
Grant me a perfect end,
your holy presence,
a blessed resurrection,
and life everlasting.
Amen.

79. FOR JUSTICE AND PEACE
(based on 1988 Constitutions)

Lord God,
you so loved the world
that you sent your only Son
that we might have life and have it abundantly.
In the fullness of time
the Lord Jesus came among us, anointed by the Spirit,
to inaugurate a kingdom of justice, love, and peace.
His rule would be no mere earthly regime;
it would initiate a new creation in every land.
His power would be within and without,
rescuing us from the injustice we suffer
and also from the injustice we inflict.
In this present time
grant to all the members of the Congregation of
    Holy Cross
and to all those with, among, and for whom we minister
the anointing of your Spirit
so that like Jesus, your Son,
we may bring good news to the poor,
release for prisoners,
sight for the blind,
and restoration for every broken victim.

We ask this through Christ our Lord.
Amen.

80. FOR THE POOR AND THE OPPRESSED

Heavenly Father,
you sent your Son
to bring good news to the poor, release for prisoners,
sight for the blind, and restoration for every victim.
I ask you in the name of Jesus Christ
to defend the cause of the weak and powerless,
and to maintain the rights of the poor and
   oppressed in our world.

Fill us, in Holy Cross, with your zeal
to come to those who are rejected, despised, and
   persecuted,
not just as servants, but as neighbors,
to be with them and of them.

May our solidarity with those in need
be a visible sign of reconciliation
which you have given us through Jesus Christ, your Son,
who with you and the Holy Spirit
lives and reign forever and ever.
Amen.

81. FOR GIVING THANKS TO GOD FOR THE GIFT OF HUMAN LIFE

(from the Roman Missal)

God our Creator,
we give thanks to you,
who alone have the power to impart the breath of life
as you form each of us in our mother's womb;
grant, we pray,
that we, whom you have made stewards of creation,
may remain faithful to this sacred trust
and constant in safeguarding the dignity of every
    human life.
Through our Lord Jesus Christ, your Son,
who lives and reigns with you in the unity of the
    Holy Spirit,
one God, forever and ever.

82. FOR THE SICK

Merciful Saint Joseph, hope of the sick,
the power of Jesus is in your hand.
Nothing is impossible to you.
If you but say the word,
the sick will be healed.

Comforter of those who invoke you with
    confidence,
listen to our prayers.
The sick have a special right to your compassion.
Lighten the pains of those we recommend to you;
grant to them the grace to sanctify their sufferings
through patience and submission to God's will.
May they be healed by your blessing
to live a holy life, completely pleasing to God.

Great Saint Joseph,
hear our prayers, increase our confidence in you,
and make us ever grateful for your blessings.

We ask this in the name of Jesus the Lord.
Amen.

---

83. FOR FAMILIES

Provident God,
we ask you to bless every family
with material, communal, and spiritual gifts
that are needed to dwell together
in a communion of love
that manifests the dignity that you desire
for all your sons and daughters.

Bless every family with a generous and hospitable spirit
toward the poor and afflicted
so that all people will come to believe
in your desire to gather all into the family of the redeemed.

Bless the families of all Holy Cross religious and my family
with an abundance of your gifts in this life
and with the fullness of eternal life in your
    kingdom.

Grant this through Christ our Lord.
Amen.

Sacred Heart of Jesus,
    —*Enfold every family in the embrace of your love.*

Our Lady of Sorrows,
    —*Pray for all families burdened by sorrow.*

Saint Joseph,
    —*Pray for God's fatherly care upon all families.*

84. LITANY OF SAINTS

Lord, have mercy	Lord, have mercy
Christ, have mercy	Christ, have mercy
Lord, have mercy	Lord, have mercy

Holy Mary, Mother of God	pray for us
Saint Michael	pray for us
Holy angels of God	pray for us
Saint John the Baptist	pray for us
Saint Peter and Saint Paul	pray for us
Saint Andrew	pray for us
Saint John	pray for us
Saint Mary Magdalene	pray for us
Saint Stephen	pray for us
Saint Ignatius of Antioch	pray for us
Saint Lawrence	pray for us
Saint Perpetua and Saint Felicity	pray for us
Saint Agnes	pray for us
Saint Gregory	pray for us
Saint Augustine	pray for us
Saint Athanasius	pray for us
Saint Basil	pray for us
Saint Martin	pray for us
Saint Benedict	pray for us
Saint Francis and Saint Dominic	pray for us
Saint Francis Xavier	pray for us
Saint John Vianney	pray for us

Saint Catherine	pray for us
Saint Teresa of Jesus	pray for us
Saint André Bessette	pray for us
Blessed Basil Moreau	pray for us
Blessed Marie-Léonie Paradis	pray for us
All holy men and women	pray for us

Lord, be merciful	Lord, deliver us, we pray
From all evil	Lord, deliver us, we pray
From every sin	Lord, deliver us, we pray
From everlasting death	Lord, deliver us, we pray
By your coming as man	Lord, deliver us, we pray
By your death and rising to new life	Lord, deliver us, we pray
By your gift of the Holy Spirit	Lord, deliver us, we pray

Be merciful to us sinners	Lord, we ask you, hear our prayer
Guide and protect your holy Church	Lord, we ask you, hear our prayer
Keep the pope and all the clergy in faithful service to your Church	Lord, we ask you, hear our prayer
Bring all peoples together in trust and peace	Lord, we ask you, hear our prayer
Strengthen us in your service	Lord, we ask you, hear our prayer
Jesus, Son of the living God	Lord, we ask you, hear our prayer

Christ, hear us
Christ, graciously hear us

Christ, hear us
Christ, graciously
   hear us

Let us pray.

God of our ancestors who set their hearts on you,
of those who fell asleep in peace,
and of those who won the martyrs' violent crown:
we are surrounded by these witnesses
as by clouds of fragrant incense.
In this age we would be counted
in this communion of all the saints;
keep us always in their good and blessed company.
In their midst we make every prayer
through Christ who is our Lord forever and ever.
Amen.

✢ VII ✢
Principal Patrons

THE FEASTS of the liturgical year will unite some of us as a community but call others away. Our own feasts, however, should give all of us the occasions as a family to pray and celebrate together. Chief among these is the solemnity of Our Lady of Sorrows, the day of remembrance in the entire congregation, for she is the patroness of us all. We celebrate also the solemnities of the Sacred Heart and of Saint Joseph, the principal feasts of the priests and brothers. (*Constitution* 3:29)

The prayers that follow are intended to foster and deepen our devotion to our special patrons.

✠ ✠ ✠ ✠ ✠ ✠ ✠

Saint Joseph

*(from a sermon by Basil Moreau
on Saint Joseph, Notre-Dame de Sainte-Croix,
March 19, 1847)*

"THE GOSPEL and tradition are extraordinarily silent about the virtues of Saint Joseph. But, would you believe that this silence tells me much more and renders our incomparable patron even greater in my eyes? How is that? The person who keeps himself hidden is truly virtuous and worthy of greater esteem than the one who exalts himself and tells the world about his wonderful deeds in order to gain the world's admiration. Such a person deserves the same praise the apostle gives to the first Christians: You have died, and now the life you have is hidden with Christ in God. But when Christ is revealed—and he is your life—you, too, will be revealed with him in glory (Col 3:3–4). What wonderful things our saint could reveal to people on earth!"

85. *Memorare* in Honor of Saint Joseph

Remember, O most chaste spouse of the Virgin Mary,
that never has it been known that anyone who
    asked for your help
and sought your intercession was left unaided.
Full of confidence in your power,
I hasten to you, and beg your protection.
Listen, O foster-father of the Redeemer,
to my humble prayer,
and in your goodness hear and answer me.
Amen.

86. Consecration to Saint Joseph

Saint Joseph, head of the Holy Family,
God chose you among men
to be the protector of the Christ Child
and the guardian of the Virgin Mary.
To you whom the Church honors as her patron
we joyfully come to consecrate ourselves
and to be your adopted children.
We feel the great need of your kind protection.

Our weakness and proneness to evil
would cause us to perish,
but for your protecting arm.

Saint Joseph,
from heaven where you reign with Jesus and Mary,
look upon us who promise to follow your example.
Grant that, after fulfilling our Christian duties on earth,
we may have the happiness of dying
with your name and the names of Jesus and Mary
on our lips.
Amen.

87. PRAYER TO SAINT JOSEPH
(especially after the recitation of the Rosary)

To you, O blessed Joseph,
we have recourse in our afflictions,
and, having implored the help of your holy Spouse,
we now, with hearts filled with confidence,
earnestly beg you also to take us under your
          protection.

By that charity with which you were united
to the Immaculate Virgin Mother of God,

and by that fatherly love with which you cherished
 the Child Jesus,
we beseech you and we humbly pray
that you will look down with gracious eyes
upon that inheritance which Jesus Christ purchased
 by his blood,
and will assist us in our need by your power and
 strength.

Defend, O most watchful guardian of the Holy Family,
the chosen offspring of Jesus Christ.
Keep from us, O most loving Father,
all error and corruption.
Aid us from on high, most valiant defender,
in this conflict with the powers of darkness.
And even as of old you rescued the Child Jesus
from the perils of his life,
so now defend God's holy Church
from the snares of the enemy and from all adversity.

Shield us ever under your patronage
that, following your example and strengthened by
 your help,
we may live a holy life, die a happy death,
and attain to everlasting bliss in heaven.
Amen.

88. To Obtain a Special Favor

O Blessed Saint Joseph,
tender-hearted father, faithful guardian of Jesus,
chaste spouse of the Mother of God,
I pray to you to join with me in praising God the Father
through his divine Son who died on the Cross
and rose again to give us sinners new life.
Through the holy Name of Jesus,
pray with us that we may obtain from the eternal Father
the favor we ask for . . .
We have been unfaithful to the unfailing love of
    God the Father;
beg of Jesus mercy for us all.
Amid the splendors of God's loving presence,
do not forget the sorrows of those who suffer,
those who pray,
those of your most holy Spouse, our Blessed Lady;
may the love of Jesus answer our call of confident
    hope.
Amen.

✠ ✠ ✠ ✠ ✠ ✠ ✠ ✠

When you invoke Saint Joseph, you don't have to speak
much. You know your Father in heaven knows what you
need. Well—so does his friend, Saint Joseph.

—**Saint André Bessette**

✠ ✠ ✠ ✠ ✠ ✠ ✠ ✠

89. FOR VOCATIONS TO HOLY CROSS

Blessed Joseph, spouse of the Mother of God,
protector of the Lord Jesus, and patron of our community,
we ask your intercession before our gracious God.

You, who are most profound in humility,
firm in faith and hope, sincere in your love,
and pure in all things, pray for us.

Great Joseph, pray for Holy Cross
that we will be blessed with new members
so we can continue the mission of Jesus
and complete God's will for us.

May we live in such a way
that we are worthy of new members.
Pray that we may grow in love for one another,

in faith of Jesus Christ, in hope for the kingdom of God.
Saint Joseph, hear our prayer and answer us.
Amen.

---

90. PRAYER TO SAINT JOSEPH, PATRON OF HOLY CROSS
(adapted from the 1947 Directory)

We pray to you, Saint Joseph,
as our powerful protector and intercessor with God,
and as the patron and benefactor of Holy Cross.

With confidence, we pray
that you will bless and protect us during this life,
and at the hour of our death.
Teach us to live with the interior spirit
and the virtues of the Holy Child, Jesus.
Glorious Joseph, protect forever our Congregation;
bless and inspire those who govern it.

Graciously look upon this community
and on all our religious wherever they may be;
increase our number with those who will glorify God;
and keep us ever faithful to our religious life.

Protect also all those who honor you,
and bless in abundance those who do good to us.

Guide us all to life everlasting.
Saint Joseph, pray for us.
Amen.

---

91. PRAYERS TO SAINT JOSEPH

(from the Votive Chapel of Saint Joseph's Oratory, Montréal, Canada)

Joseph, Our Solace in Suffering

Compassionate Joseph, one with us in our human
    condition,
together with Mary and Jesus you experienced
    exile, hunger, and violence.
Refusing vengeance, you choose mercy.
Your forgiveness breaks the circle of violence.
Through your goodness, God's hope for our
    humanity is preserved.
Joy is yours, for the kingdom of God is your
    inheritance.
Open our compassionate hands in times of war,
    famine, and exile.
Keep us from developing a victim's mentality,
and make our pain a source of growth.
Sustain us in fulfilling our responsibility of
    cultivating inner peace, joy, and serenity.
In your wisdom, counsel us to close all doors to bitterness,

so that, watched over by God, we may dance for
    joy.
Amen.

Joseph, Model of Laborers

Good Saint Joseph,
when God wanted a family for his Son,
he looked among the laborers, and chose you along
    with Mary,
demonstrating his esteem for human work.
You put your heart into your work,
and shared your workshop with Jesus.
Your work, like that of others,
found new meaning in the presence of God.
Sustain us in the hope of finding work
when we are confronted with the desolation of
    unemployment.
Counsel business leaders to create an equitable
    division of labor
that is respectful of individuals and promotes our
    growth and happiness.
Help us to perform our work joyfully,
    conscientiously, fairly, and honestly.
Prepare our hearts to recognize your Son in our
    colleagues at work.
Amen.

Joseph, Mainstay of Families

Attentive Joseph,
in Mary and you, the Divine Word finds a favorable
　　environment
in which to carry out the will of the Father;
thus, you become the family of the Child-God.
In your gentle life together, you experience love daily.
The unity of your hearts transforms life's lessons
into growing wisdom and grace.
Open our hearts to the Word that lives within us,
that our actions may bear witness to our connection
　　to the family of God.
Sustain us in our emotional commitments,
where giving and forgiveness shape our identities.
Grant us your tenderness in the things we do each
　　day!
Amen.

Joseph, Hope of the Sick

Benevolent Joseph,
the Son of God placed his life in your hands.
With Mary, you cared for him who is the force of life.
May your compassion enfold our fragility,
bringing us the comfort of the divine presence.
We join with you in prayer, saying,

"Lord Jesus, Son of the Living God, say a word for
    our healing!"
Make us sensitive to the illnesses of those close to us.
Support our efforts and grant us courage in the
    fight against all evil.
Help us to find meaning in God's great plan for humanity
    beyond the sicknesses and sufferings that blind our sight.
The love of God be with us, as our hope lies with him!
Amen.

When praying with the sick or recommending prayers for the sick,
it was the common practice of Brother André to encourage the use
of holy oil as a sign of God's power and desire to heal. For the Rite
of Anointing within Mass, see Ritual Prayer, *Part I, D.*

Joseph, Patron of the Dying

Faithful Joseph,
with the fulfillment of the Lord's promise,
you peacefully leave this world in Jesus' and Mary's hands.
Your faith transforms death into the sowing of life;
thus, God considers you to be a just man.
Your heart overflows in the presence of the Lord.
With your hands outstretched to God, your night is
    filled with prayers.
Surrounded by the living,
you embark upon the great march to the promised land.
Open our eyes that we may glimpse the road to life
    that lies beyond death.

May nothing, not denial, anger, nor depression,
separate us from the love of God.
Strengthen our faith in God, who always finds ways
of preserving us in his friendship.
Stay beside us to hold our hands
when we take our first steps toward the eternal
  kingdom.
Amen.

Joseph, Protector of the Church

Brave Joseph, collaborator in God's plan for humanity,
your tenderness enfolds the newborn Church.
Just as Mary and Jesus recognize in you the
  protection of the Father,
so too does the community of faith place itself
  under your protection.
Strengthen us with the Spirit that filled the
  Nazarene home,
and guide our footsteps on the road to the kingdom.
Accompany us in carrying out our mission.
Help us to be lights in the world so that the family
  of God
may spring forth from humanity transfigured in Christ.
Grant us the strength to imitate God's preference
  for the poor and weak.
Guide us in our pastoral activities

that our actions may be modeled on the Good
   News.
Amen.

Joseph, Terror of Demons

Courageous Joseph,
advised by an angel,
you confronted your fears of the unknown.
Your light shines brightly, penetrating the dark
   corners of your being.
Your fears dispersed, you rediscovered your true face,
and actively participated in the divine plan,
reuniting mother and Child, and the people with
   their God.
Together with Mary and Jesus, you dwell in the
   love of God.
Help us to rediscover the united core
of our identities beyond all internal fears.
Counsel us so we may build a better world
to welcome the coming kingdom.
Shed your light on our inner lives
that, freed from the grip of our fears,
our decisions may be founded in love.
May the face of God shine on us!
Amen.

Joseph, Guardian of the Pure of Heart

Gentle Joseph,
God is captivated by the quality of your heart.
Your entire being is focused on doing his will.
With Mary and Jesus, you answer the Holy Spirit's
  call to build a better world.
With one heart, we join you in saying,
"Here we are, Lord, your will be done!
Your kingdom come nearer to us!"
Keep the hope of a new world alive in our hearts.
Inspire us to speak words of tenderness to awaken
  the love of hearts.
May we draw the energy for our actions from the
  source of all love
so our faces may shine with the freedom of the
  children of God.
Amen.

92. THE JOYS AND SORROWS OF SAINT JOSEPH

For each joy and sorrow, the pertinent scripture passage is
referenced in full. For reasons of space, only a few selected
verses are presented here for mysteries I–V.

I. Joseph's Worries during His Engagement

(see Matthew 1:18–24)

"An angel of the Lord appeared to him in a dream and said, 'Joseph, son of David, do not be afraid to take Mary as your wife, for the child conceived in her is from the Holy Spirit. She will bear a son, and you are to name him Jesus, for he will save his people from their sins.'"

Meditation

Saint Joseph, we can scarcely imagine your affliction and anguish when you were aware that Mary your betrothed was expecting a child whose origin was unknown to you. Your confidence in her prevented you from condemning her and your righteousness from putting her to shame. Staring into such a great mystery, you considered whether it was better to go your way, and it was with extreme pain that you were about to send her away in secret, believing that your union with her was forever doomed.

But the news the angel delivered in your sleep allowed you to understand that the Messiah had just become flesh by the Holy Spirit in the Virgin Mary; not only was Mary blessed by God, but you also were to keep her as your wife and Jesus, the Son of God, as your son. With what joy and respect

you must have responded to the angel's order, and
with what bliss you were ready to live with Mary and
Jesus, the two holiest beings that ever existed.

Prayer

With this example before our eyes, O Saint Joseph,
we ask you to grant that we may understand
that in our lives great graces may come after great trials,
and that when sorrow visits us
it does not mean that God forsakes us
but rather that he is near,
preparing us solace after suffering, in his goodness.

Our Father. Hail Mary. Glory be.

II. The Birth of Jesus and the Adoration of the Shepherds

(see Luke 2:1–20)

"Joseph went from the town of Nazareth in Galilee
to Judea, to the city of David called Bethlehem,
because he was descended from the house and family of David. He went to be registered with Mary,
to whom he was engaged and who was expecting a
child. While they were there, the time came for her
to deliver her child.

"The angel said to the shepherds, 'Do not be
afraid; for see, I am bringing you good news of

great joy for all the people: to you is born this day
in the city of David a Savior, who is the Messiah, the
Lord.' The shepherds said to one another, 'Let us go
now to Bethlehem and see this thing that has taken
place.' So they went with haste and found Mary and
Joseph, and the child lying in the manger."

Meditation

Saint Joseph, your surprise and sorrow must
have been great when on your way to Bethlehem
you were refused a place in the inn, just at the time
when Mary, about to give birth to the Messiah, was
in need of rest and privacy. Undoubtedly, it must
have taken you much faith and hope to accept such
miserable conditions for the birth of the Son of God,
remarkable for its destitution and neglect. But your
sorrow was changed into joy and your suffering
into hope when you saw the shepherds, sent by the
angels, arrive at the manger to adore the Son of God.

Prayer

Saint Joseph,
obtain for us the grace to understand
that our faith is often put to the test,
that we must meet all obstacles with strength and
     perseverance,
and that God reaches out for us
not in riches or pomp but in poverty and humility.

Our Father. Hail Mary. Glory be.

III. Presentation of Jesus in the Temple
(see Luke 2:22–40)

"When the time came for their purification according to the law of Moses, Mary and Joseph brought him up to Jerusalem to present him to the Lord (as it is written in the law of the Lord, 'Every firstborn male shall be designated as holy to the Lord'), and they offered a sacrifice according to what is stated in the law of the Lord, 'a pair of turtle-doves or two young pigeons.'

"And the child's father and mother were amazed at what was being said about him. When they had finished everything required by the law of the Lord, they returned to Galilee, to their own town of Nazareth. The child grew and became strong, filled with wisdom; and the favor of God was upon him."

Meditation

Saint Joseph, when you went up to the Temple with the Virgin Mary and her son Jesus, you wanted to fulfill both the prescriptions for the purification of the Mother and offering of the Child. It was a great joy when you saw that Simeon and Anna, by prophetic inspiration, recognized the Messiah in Jesus and sang his praise and his future glory. But just as for Mary, a sword pierced through your soul when you heard that Jesus must fulfill his mission and save humanity through suffering and that he was destined to bring about the fall and the rise of many in Israel.

Prayer

Saint Joseph,
by these joys and sorrows of yours,
help us to recognize that God may at times
take away the gifts he has bestowed on us,
and teach us to bless and love him,
even when he sends tribulations after rejoicing.

Our Father. Hail Mary. Glory be.

IV. The Visit of the Wise Men and Flight into Egypt

(see Matthew 2:1–15)

"When the magi saw that the star had stopped, they were overwhelmed with joy. On entering the house, they saw the child with Mary his mother; and they knelt down and paid him homage.

"Now after they had left, an angel of the Lord appeared to Joseph in a dream and said, 'Get up, take the child and his mother, and flee to Egypt, and remain there until I tell you; for Herod is about to search for the child, to destroy him.' Then Joseph got up, took the child and his mother by night, and went to Egypt, and remained there until the death of Herod."

Meditation

Saint Joseph, after the purification of Mary and the presentation of Jesus in the Temple, you had the joy of seeing another testimony to the divinity and mission of Jesus. The wise men from the East brought before him their gifts and homage. So, after the humble shepherds, representing the Jewish people, were called, the wise men from the East, representing all nations, had been summoned. But the sword of affliction was drawn: Herod, hearing of a newborn King of the Jews and fearing for his rank, decided to put the Child to death. Warned in a dream, you had to leave for a foreign country with Mary and the child.

Prayer

Saint Joseph,
we beseech you, help us to imitate you wholeheartedly
when we are subjected, against our will and fancy,
to the mysterious and disarming action of Divine
    Providence.
Make us understand that "the ways of God are not
    our ways,"
and that what we think wise and essential
may appear to him as silly and dangerous to our souls.

Grant that we accept, as you did,
these contradictions that escape our understanding
but can lead us back to the way of grace and
    salvation.

Our Father. Hail Mary. Glory be.

V. Jesus Lost and Found

(see Luke 2:41–52)

"When his parents saw him they were astonished;
and his mother said to him, 'Child, why have you
treated us like this? Look, your father and I have
been searching for you in great anxiety.' He said to
them, 'Why were you searching for me? Did you not
know that I must be in my Father's house?' But they
did not understand what he said to them. Then he
went down with them and came to Nazareth, and
was obedient to them. His mother treasured all these
things in her heart."

Meditation

Saint Joseph, how troubled and anguished you
must have been when, returning from Jerusalem,
you became aware with Mary that the child God
had entrusted to you was no longer with you. What
eagerness in your search for him during three days!
What happiness in finding him in the Temple and

coming back to Nazareth where he lived with you in peace and subjection, advancing in favor and wisdom and working at your side.

Prayer

Obtain for us the grace, O Saint Joseph,
to seek our Savior with your eagerness and Mary's.
Teach us to find him in the Temple
in the midst of teachers,
that is, in the Eucharist and in the teaching of
 God's Church.
Make us experience the happiness of living with him
in peace and conformably to God's will,
that we also may grow in favor and in wisdom.

Our Father. Hail Mary. Glory be.

VI. The Joys and Sorrows of Joseph at Work

(see Matthew 13:53–55)

"When Jesus had finished these parables, he left that place. He came to his hometown and began to teach the people in their synagogue, so that they were astounded and said, 'Where did this man get this wisdom and these deeds of power? Is not this the carpenter's son?'"

Meditation

Saint Joseph, when we learn from the Gospel that you were a carpenter, we understand that your life was spent in the humble and patient labor of the workers of all times. In this daily work which you did wholeheartedly to earn the living of the Holy Family, you surely met with joy and sorrow, trial and solace. Hours of success and gain were followed by hours of sickness and fatigue. You met generous and polite customers but also exacting and churlish ones. Some chores were pleasant and easy; others, difficult and thankless. But in every situation you did your best and fulfilled your obligations.

Prayer

Teach us, O Saint Joseph,
to fulfill our daily tasks with perfection,
to work for God and not only for people,
with care and honesty,
and to accept contradiction and rejoicing in a
    Christian spirit.

Our Father. Hail Mary. Glory be.

VII. Death of Saint Joseph
(see John 19:26–27)

"When Jesus saw his mother and the disciple whom he loved standing beside her, he said to his mother, 'Woman, here is your son.' Then he said to the disciple, 'Here is your mother.' And from that hour the disciple took her into his own home."

Meditation

Saint Joseph, we do not know the circumstances of your death. But since Jesus, dying on the Cross, asked his beloved disciple to look after Mary, the Church has always believed that you had the joy of dying in the arms of Jesus and Mary. That is why the Church sees in you the patron of the dying. After a holy life, you died a happy death, and after the trials of this life, you experienced the bliss of heaven where you now enjoy the presence of Jesus and Mary.

Prayer

Saint Joseph,
who experienced the joy of dying
in the embrace of Jesus and Mary
and whom Christians honor
as the patron and comforter of the dying,
we call on you today for your protection
at the last moment of our life.

May we die the death of the just,
and in order to merit such a grace,
may we live like you in the presence of the Lord
and the Virgin Mary,
so as to share in the redemption
when we appear for the judgment of the Lord.

Our Father. Hail Mary. Glory be.

✦ ✦ ✦ ✦ ✦ ✦ ✦

Do not seek to have your trials lifted from you. Instead,
ask for the grace to bear them well.

—**Saint André Bessette**

✦ ✦ ✦ ✦ ✦ ✦ ✦

93. PRAYER TO SAINT JOSEPH FOR A
HAPPY DEATH (I)

O blessed Joseph,
who died in the arms of Jesus and Mary,
obtain for me, I beseech you,
the grace of a happy death.
In that hour when I shall pass
from this life to eternity,

assist me by your presence,
and protect me by your power
against the enemies of my salvation.
Into your hands, living and dying,
and of those of Jesus and Mary,
I commend my spirit.
Amen.

---

94. Prayer to Saint Joseph for a Happy Death (II)

Saint Joseph,
who had the joy of dying between Jesus and Mary,
and whom Christians honor
as the patron and comforter of the dying,
I call upon your protection
at the last moments of my life.
May I die the death of the just,
and to obtain such a grace
may I live as you in the presence
of the Lord and of the Virgin Mary,
so as to share in the redemption
when I also will have to appear before God.
Amen.

95. LITANY OF SAINT JOSEPH

Lord, have mercy	Lord, have mercy
Christ, have mercy	Christ, have mercy
Lord, have mercy	Lord, have mercy
God our Father in heaven	have mercy on us
God the Son, Redeemer of the world	have mercy on us
God the Holy Spirit	have mercy on us
Holy Trinity, one God	have mercy on us
Holy Mary	pray for us
Saint Joseph	pray for us
Noble son of the House of David	pray for us
Light of patriarchs	pray for us
Husband of the Mother of God	pray for us
Guardian of the Virgin	pray for us
Foster father of the Son of God	pray for us
Faithful guardian of Christ	pray for us
Head of the Holy Family	pray for us
Joseph, chaste and just	pray for us
Joseph, prudent and brave	pray for us
Joseph, obedient and loyal	pray for us
Pattern of patience	pray for us
Lover of poverty	pray for us
Model of workers	pray for us
Example to parents	pray for us

Guardian of virgins	pray for us
Pillar of family life	pray for us
Comfort of the troubled	pray for us
Hope of the sick	pray for us
Patron of the dying	pray for us
Terror of evil spirits	pray for us
Protector of the Church	pray for us

Lamb of God, you take away
   the sins of the world   have mercy on us
Lamb of God, you take away
   the sins of the world   have mercy on us
Lamb of God, you take away
   the sins of the world   have mercy on us

God made him master of his household.
   —*And ruler of all his possessions.*

Let us pray.

O God,
you were pleased to choose Saint Joseph
as the husband of Mary and the guardian of your Son.
Grant that, as we venerate him as our protector on earth,
we may deserve to have him as our intercessor in heaven.
We ask this through Christ our Lord.
Amen.

✤ ✤ ✤ ✤ ✤ ✤ ✤ ✤

The Blessed Virgin Mary, Our Lady of Sorrows

(from a sermon by Basil Moreau on the Heart of Mary, February 8, 1841)

"YOU ALL know what we mean when we speak of a mother's love, the love a mother has for the children she bore, a love that makes her think constantly about them and to work for this happiness. What is more tender, stronger, more generous, and more heroic? This is only a feeble image of what Mary's heart feels for each of us and of the love that burns there for us since she became our mother and adopted us as her children. It is here that you can glimpse the excess of her tenderness as you witness everything she suffered to make us happy for all eternity."

---

96. *MEMORARE*

Remember, O most gracious Virgin Mary,
that never was it known

that anyone who fled to thy protection,
implored thy help,
or sought thy intercession
was left unaided.
Inspired by this confidence
I fly unto thee, O Virgin of virgins, my Mother.
To thee do I come,
before thee I stand, sinful and sorrowful.
O Mother of the Word Incarnate,
despise not my petitions,
but in thy mercy hear and answer me.
Amen.

---

97. *Sub Tuum Præsidium*

We fly to thy protection,
O holy Mother of God;
despise not our petitions in our necessities,
but deliver us always from all dangers,
O glorious and blessed Virgin.

---

98. An Ancient Prayer to Our Lady

O Mother of God,
we take refuge in your loving care.

Let not our plea to you pass unheeded
in the trials that beset us,
but deliver us from danger,
for you alone are truly pure,
you alone are truly blessed.

99. TOTA PULCHRA ES

You are all beautiful, Mary,
and there is no original stain in you.

100. CONSECRATION TO THE BLESSED VIRGIN MARY
(1859 Directory)

O my Mother and Patroness, Holy Mary,
I deliver myself to your faithful protection and your
    special care,
now, for every day, and at the hour of my death.
I seek refuge in the bosom of your mercy,
and I entrust my body and soul to you.
I entrust all my hopes and consolations,
all my sufferings and miseries, my life and its end,
that through your most holy intercession and your merits
all my works may be directed and performed
according to your will and that of your Son.

O my Lady! O my Mother!
I wholly offer myself to you, and to give you a
    proof of my love,
I now consecrate to you my eyes, my mouth, my
    ears, my heart, and in a word my whole being.
Since therefore I am yours, O Good Mother,
preserve and defend me as your own possession.
Amen.

101. VOCATION PRAYER TO MARY, MOTHER OF SORROWS

Hail Mary, full of grace, all generations call you
    blessed.

Hail Mary, Mother of Sorrows,
upon hearing the prophecy of Simeon, a sword
    pierced your heart.
Comfort those discerning God's call,
that to follow your Son as a Holy Cross priest,
    brother, or sister
is not just demanding, but joy filled.

Hail Mary, Mother of Sorrows,
you made the journey to Egypt with Joseph
to ensure your Son's safety.

Give courage and perseverance to those
who find the journey of discernment unsettling.
Assure them that God will eventually lead them
    safely home.

Hail Mary, Mother of Sorrows,
you searched for your Son, Jesus, in the Temple.
Be with those who search for God's truth in their lives.
Lead them to the light of his will.

Hail Mary, Mother of Sorrows,
on the road to Calvary your eyes of compassion
    lovingly looked upon your Son.
Turn your gentle gaze upon those contemplating
    his footsteps.
May they be inspired by the example and witness
of a "great band of men" in Holy Cross
who walk side by side in their following of the
    Lord.

Hail Mary, Mother of Sorrows, at the foot of the Cross,
you witnessed your Son's total giving of self to the Father.
Strengthen those who wish to abandon all in his
    holy name.

Hail Mary, Mother of Sorrows,
you lovingly embraced the lifeless body

of your Son, Jesus Christ, after his crucifixion.
Hold close to your heart those in the Congregation
whose vocations suffer from listlessness and apathy.

Hail Mary, Mother of Sorrows,
you were present when Jesus' body was laid in the tomb.
Encourage those discerning religious life in Holy Cross
to lay their fears at the feet of your Son,
confident in the hope and promise of new life.

Hail Mary, full of grace,
may future generations of Holy Cross religious call
    you blessed.
Amen.

---

102. The Chaplet of Our Lady of Sorrows

Father Moreau entrusted to his beloved daughters, the Marianites of Holy Cross, the daily recitation of the Chaplet of Our Lady of the Seven Dolors.
Although Moreau did not entrust this practice to his
beloved sons, he invited them in meditating on the
Stations of the Cross to "follow Mary in the sorrowful way, sympathizing with her afflicted heart"
(*1859 Directory*). As we draw near to our patroness
in her way of sorrow, we ask that our hearts might

be opened to all whose daily lives bear the marks of suffering and who yearn for the redemption won for all by the Cross of Christ.

The Rosary of Our Lady of the Seven Sorrows consists of seven mysteries. Each mystery begins with a brief scripture passage recounting a sorrow of Mary. The Our Father (on the medal that depicts the mystery) is said, followed by seven Hail Marys. After the completion of the seven mysteries, three Hail Marys are prayed in memory of her tear-filled sorrows.

I. The Prophecy of Simeon

(for those who carry hidden and difficult burdens)

"This child is destined for the falling and the rising of many in Israel, and to be a sign that will be opposed so that the inner thoughts of many will be revealed—and a sword will pierce your own soul too." (Lk 2:34)

Our Father, seven Hail Marys (after each scripture reflection)

II. The Flight into Egypt

(for refugees, migrant workers, and immigrants)

"Get up, take the child and his mother, and flee to Egypt, and remain there until I tell you, for Herod is about to search for the child, to destroy him." (Mt 2:13b)

III. The Loss of the Child Jesus in the Temple

(for children who are victimized and abused)

"When they did not find him, they returned to Jerusalem to search for him." (Lk 2:45)

IV. Mary Meets Jesus Carrying the Cross

(for those who accompany the suffering with compassion)

"A great number of the people followed him, and among them were women who were beating their breasts and wailing for him." (Lk 23:27)

V. Mary at the Foot of the Cross

(for victims of violence, war, and capital punishment)

"When Jesus saw his mother and the disciple whom he loved standing beside her, he said to his mother, 'Woman, here is your son.' Then he said to the disciple, 'Here is your mother.'" (Jn 19:26–27)

VI. Mary Receives the Body of Jesus in Her Arms

(for those who mourn)

"My soul melts away for sorrow; strengthen me according to your word." (Ps 119:28)

VII. The Burial of Jesus

(for the gift of hope for the despairing)

"So Joseph took the body and wrapped it in a clean linen cloth and laid it in his own new tomb, which he had hewn in the rock." (Mt 27:59–60)

Following the usual Our Father and seven Hail Marys, a final three Hail Marys are said in memory of Mary's tear-filled sorrows.

---

103. THE ROSARY OF THE BLESSED VIRGIN MARY

In calling the members of the Congregation to the daily praying of the Rosary, Basil Moreau emphasized the necessity of meditating upon its mysteries by calling to mind the "life of Jesus Christ" and the usefulness of asking for "a grace or a virtue corresponding to the mystery which ought to be meditated" (*1859 Directory*). The virtues ascribed to the

Joyful, Sorrowful, and Glorious Mysteries are those suggested by Father Moreau in the *1859 Directory*. The Luminous Mysteries were added by Pope John Paul II in 2002.

The Rosary begins with the Sign of the Cross, followed by the Apostles' Creed.

The Apostles' Creed

I believe in God, the Father almighty, Creator of heaven and earth, and in Jesus Christ, his only Son, our Lord, who was conceived by the Holy Spirit, born of the Virgin Mary, suffered under Pontius Pilate, was crucified, died, and was buried; he descended into hell; on the third day he rose again from the dead; he ascended into heaven, and is seated at the right hand of God, the Father almighty; from there he will come to judge the living and the dead. I believe in the Holy Spirit, the holy catholic Church, the communion of saints, the forgiveness of sins, the resurrection of the body, and life everlasting. Amen.

Joyful Mysteries (Monday and Saturday)

I
The Annunciation
(Humility)

"Here am I, the servant of the Lord, let it be done with me according to your word." (Lk 1:38)

II
The Visitation
(Fraternal Charity)

"And why has this happened to me, that the mother of my Lord comes to me?" (Lk 1:43)

III
The Nativity
(Love of Poverty)

"And she gave birth to her first-born son and wrapped him in bands of cloth, and laid him in a manger because there was no place for them in the inn." (Lk 2:7)

IV
The Presentation in the Temple
(Fidelity to Chastity)

"For my eyes have seen your salvation, which you have prepared in the presence of all people, a light for revelation to the Gentiles and for glory to your people Israel." (Lk 2:30–31)

V
The Finding of the Child Jesus in the Temple
(Zeal for Souls)

"Why were you searching for me? Did you not know that I must be in my Father's house." (Lk 2:49)

Sorrowful Mysteries (Tuesday and Friday)

I
The Agony in the Garden
(Gift of Meditation and Contrition)

"Could you not keep awake one hour? Keep awake and pray that you may not come into the time of trial." (Mk 14:37b–38a)

II
The Scourging
(Patience)

"So Pilate, wishing to satisfy the crowds, released Barabbas for them; and after flogging Jesus, he handed him over to be crucified." (Mk 15:15)

III

The Crowning with Thorns
(Mortification)

"After twisting some thorns into a crown, they put it on him. And they began saluting him, 'Hail, King of the Jews.'" (Mk 15:17b–18)

IV

The Carrying of the Cross
(Grace to Bear One's Cross)

"After mocking him, they stripped him of his purple cloak and put his own clothes on him. Then they led him out to crucify him." (Mk 15:20)

V

The Crucifixion
(Obedience)

"He saved others, he cannot save himself. Let the Messiah, the King of Israel, come down from that cross now, so that we may see and believe." (Mk 15:31b)

Glorious Mysteries (Wednesday and Saturday)

I
The Resurrection
(Renewal of the Interior Life)

"Do not be afraid; go and tell my brothers to go to Galilee; there they will see me." (Mt 28:10)

II
The Ascension
(Indifference to Worldly Things)

"Men of Galilee, why do you stand looking up towards heaven? This Jesus, who has been taken up from you into heaven, will come in the same way you saw him going into heaven." (Acts 1:11)

III
The Descent of the Holy Spirit
(Love of Solitude)

"Divided tongues, as of fire, appeared among them, and a tongue rested on each of them." (Acts 2:3)

IV
The Assumption of Mary
(Desire for Heaven)

"If for this life only we have hope in Christ, we are of all people most to be pitied. But in fact Christ has been raised from the dead, the first fruits of those who have died." (1 Cor 15:19–20)

V
The Coronation of Mary
(Final Perseverance)

"A great portent appeared in heaven: a woman clothed with the sun, with the moon under her feet, and on her head a crown of twelve stars." (Rv 12:1)

Luminous Mysteries (Thursday)

I
The Baptism of Jesus
(Reverence for All God's Beloved Children)

"And a voice from heaven said, 'This is my Son, the Beloved, with whom I am well pleased.'" (Mt 3:17)

II
The Proclamation of the Kingdom of God
(Growth as an Educator in the Faith)

"Blessed are those who hunger and thirst for righteousness, for they will be filled." (Mt 5:6)

III
The Wedding Feast at Cana
(Fidelity to the Vowed Life)

"His mother said to the servants, 'Do whatever he tells you.'" (Jn 2:5)

IV
The Transfiguration
(Sanctification of All the Members of the Family of Holy Cross)

"'This is my Son, the Beloved, with him I am well pleased!' When the disciples heard this they fell to the ground and were overcome by fear. But Jesus came and touched them saying, 'Get up and do not be afraid.'" (Mt 17:5b–7)

V
The Institution of the Eucharist
(Building Up of Christ's Body, the Church)

"This is my body, which is given for you. Do this in remembrance of me." (Lk 22:19b)

After the mysteries have been recited, the Hail, Holy Queen is said together with the concluding prayer.

Hail, Holy Queen

Hail, Holy Queen, Mother of mercy, our life, our sweetness, and our hope. To you do we cry, poor banished children of Eve. To you do we send up our sighs, mourning and weeping in this valley of tears. Turn then, most gracious advocate, your eyes of mercy towards us; and after this our exile, show unto us the blessed fruit of your womb, Jesus. O clement! O loving! O sweet Virgin Mary!

Pray for us, O Holy Mother of God,
—*That we may be made worthy of the promises of Christ.*

Let us pray.

O God,
whose only-begotten Son,
by his life, death, and resurrection,
has purchased for us the rewards of eternal life,
grant we beseech you,
that, meditating upon the mysteries
of the most holy Rosary of the Blessed Virgin Mary,

we may imitate what they contain
and obtain what they promise,
through the same Christ, our Lord.
Amen.

---

104. *ANGELUS*

The angel of the Lord declared unto Mary.
  —*And she conceived by the Holy Spirit.*

Hail Mary, full of grace, the Lord is with you;
Blessed are you among women;
and blessed is the fruit of your womb, Jesus.
  —*Holy Mary, Mother of God,*
  pray for us sinners, now and at the
  hour of our death. Amen.

Behold the handmaid of the Lord.
  —*Be it done unto me according to your word.*

Hail, Mary...

And the Word was made flesh.
  —*And dwelt among us.*

Hail, Mary...

Pray for us, O holy Mother of God.
—*That we may be made worthy of the promises of Christ.*

Let us pray.

Pour forth, we beseech you, O Lord,
your grace into our hearts,
that we, to whom the Incarnation of Christ, your
    Son,
was made known by the message of an angel,
may, by his Passion and Cross,
be brought to the glory of his Resurrection,
through the same Christ our Lord.
Amen.

---

105. Marian Anthems

Alma Redemptoris Mater

(from the First Sunday of Advent until the Presentation of the Lord)

Alma Redemptoris Mater, quæ pervia cæli
porta manes, et stella maris, succurre cadenti,
surgere qui curat, populo: tu quæ genuisti,

natura mirante, tuum sanctum Genitorem,
Virgo prius ac posterius, Gabrielis ab ore,
sumens illud Ave, peccatorum miserere.

Loving Mother of the Redeemer,
gate of heaven, star of the sea,
assist your people who have fallen
yet strive to rise again.
To the wonderment of nature you bore your Creator,
yet remained a virgin after as before.
You who received Gabriel's joyful greeting,
have pity on us poor sinners.

Ave Regina Cælorum

(from the Presentation of the Lord until Wednesday of Holy Week)

Ave, Regina cælorum,
ave, Domina angelorum,
salve, radix, salve, porta,
ex qua mundo lux est orta.

Gaude, Virgo gloriosa,
super omnes speciosa;
vale, o valde decora,
et pro nobis Christum exora.

Hail, Queen of heaven;
Hail, Mistress of the Angels;
Hail, root of Jesus;
Hail, the gate through which
the Light rose over the earth.

Rejoice, Virgin most renowned
and of unsurpassed beauty,
and pray for us to Christ.

Regina Cæli

(from Easter Sunday until Trinity Sunday)

Regina cæli lætare, alleluia:
Quia quem meruisti portare, alleluia,
Resurrexit, sicut dixit, alleluia.
Ora pro nobis Deum, alleluia.

Queen of Heaven, rejoice, alleluia;
for he whom you were chosen to bear, alleluia,
has risen as he said, alleluia;
pray for us to God, alleluia.

Salve Regina

(from Monday after Pentecost until the beginning of Advent)

Salve, Regina, Mater misericordiæ,
vita, dulcedo, et spes nostra, salve.
Ad te clamamus exsules filii Evæ,
ad te suspiramus, gementes et flentes
in hac lacrimarum valle.

Eia, ergo, advocata mostra, illos tuos
misericordes oculos ad nos converte;
et Iesum, benedictum fructum ventris tui,
nobis post hoc exilium ostende.
O clemens, O pia, O dulcis Virgo Maria.

Hail, holy Queen, Mother of mercy,
our life, our sweetness, and our hope.
To you do we cry, poor banished children of Eve;
to you we send up our sighs,
mourning and weeping in this vale of tears.

Turn, then, most gracious advocate,
your eyes of mercy toward us;
and after this, our exile,
show us the blessed fruit of your womb, Jesus.
O clement, O loving, O sweet Virgin Mary.

106. LITANY OF THE BLESSED VIRGIN MARY
(Litany of Loreto)

Lord, have mercy	Lord, have mercy
Christ, have mercy	Christ, have mercy
Lord, have mercy	Lord, have mercy
Holy Mary	pray for us
Holy Mother of God	pray for us
Most honored of virgins	pray for us
Mother of Christ	pray for us
Mother of the Church	pray for us
Mother of divine grace	pray for us
Mother most pure	pray for us
Mother of chaste love	pray for us
Mother and Virgin	pray for us
Sinless Mother	pray for us
Dearest of mothers	pray for us
Model of motherhood	pray for us
Mother of good counsel	pray for us
Mother of our Creator	pray for us
Mother of our Savior	pray for us
Virgin most wise	pray for us
Virgin rightly praised	pray for us
Virgin rightly renowned	pray for us
Virgin most powerful	pray for us
Virgin gentle in mercy	pray for us

Faithful Virgin	pray for us
Mirror of justice	pray for us
Throne of wisdom	pray for us
Cause of our joy	pray for us
Shrine of the Spirit	pray for us
Glory of Israel	pray for us
Vessel of selfless devotion	pray for us
Mystical Rose	pray for us
Tower of David	pray for us
Tower of ivory	pray for us
House of gold	pray for us
Ark of the covenant	pray for us
Morning Star	pray for us
Health of the sick	pray for us
Refuge of sinners	pray for us
Comfort of the troubled	pray for us
Help of Christians	pray for us
Queen of angels	pray for us
Queen of patriarchs and prophets	pray for us
Queen of apostles and martyrs	pray for us
Queen of confessors and virgins	pray for us
Queen of all saints	pray for us
Queen conceived without sin	pray for us
Queen assumed into heaven	pray for us
Queen of the Rosary	pray for us
Queen of families	pray for us
Queen of peace	pray for us

Lamb of God, you take away
 the sins of the world   have mercy on us
Lamb of God, you take away
 the sins of the world   have mercy on us
Lamb of God, you take away
 the sins of the world   have mercy on us

Let us pray.

Eternal God,
let your people enjoy constant health
 in mind and body.
Through the intercession of the Virgin Mary
free us from the sorrows of this life
and lead us to happiness in the life to come.
Grant this through Christ our Lord.
Amen.

✠ ✠ ✠ ✠ ✠ ✠ ✠ ✠

The Sacred Heart of Jesus

*(from a sermon by Basil Moreau
on the Sacred Heart of Jesus, 1833)*

"IT IS in our interest to practice a devotion that leads us to virtue, one that can be a source of abundant blessings. First of all, this devotion [to the Sacred Heart] leads to virtue. One of the principal goals of this devotion is to present us a model for imitation. The sight of the Savior's heart should say to each of us, as in the past when Moses was given the plan for the Ark of the Covenant and the tabernacle, 'Look at this example and make a faithful copy' (Ex 25:40). This is the heart of the One given to you as master. Your duty is to conform your heart to his."

---

107. *MEMORARE* TO THE SACRED HEART

Remember, most sweet Jesus,
that no one who has had recourse to your Sacred Heart,
implored its help, or sought its mercy
was ever abandoned.

Encouraged with confidence,
O tenderest of hearts,
we present ourselves before you,
burdened with the weight of our sins.
In our need, Sacred Heart of Jesus,
despise not our simple prayers,
but mercifully grant our requests.
Amen.

---

108. Prayer to the Sacred Heart of Jesus

Most holy Heart of Jesus,
fountain of every blessing,
I adore you and with lively sorrow for my sins
I offer you this poor heart of mine.
Make me humble, patient, pure,
and wholly obedient to your will.
Grant, good Jesus,
that I may live in you and for you;
protect me in the midst of danger;
comfort me in my afflictions.
Give me health of body,
assistance in my temporal needs,
your blessing on all that I do,
and the grace of a holy death.
Amen.

109. ACT OF CONSECRATION TO THE SACRED HEART

(Saint Margaret Mary Alacoque)

O Sacred Heart of Jesus,
to you I consecrate and offer
my person and my life, my actions, trials, and sufferings,
that my entire being may henceforth only be employed
in loving, honoring, and glorifying you.
This is my irrevocable will, to belong entirely to you,
and to do all for your love, renouncing with my
    whole heart all that can displease you.
I take you, O Sacred Heart, for the sole object of
    my love,
the protection of my life, the pledge of my salvation,
the remedy of my frailty and inconstancy,
the reparation for all the defects of my life,
and my secure refuge at the hour of my death.
Most Merciful Heart, be my justification before
    God the Father,
and protect me from his anger which I have so
    justly merited.
I fear all from my own weakness and malice,
but placing my entire confidence in you, Heart of Love,
I hope all from your infinite goodness.
Cleanse me from all that can displease or resist you.

Imprint your pure love so deeply in my heart
that I may never forget you or be separated from you.
I ask you, through your infinite goodness,
to engrave my name upon your Heart,
for in this I place all my happiness and all my glory,
to live and to die as one of your devoted servants.
Amen.

110. CONSECRATION TO THE SACRED HEART
(1947 Directory)

Lord Jesus, Redeemer of the human race,
look upon me humbly before your altar.
I am yours and yours I wish to be;
to be most surely united with you,
I ask you to see me in my weakness,
as I desire to consecrate myself today to your most
    Sacred Heart.
Many indeed have never known you;
many too, rejecting your precepts, have turned
    from you.
Have mercy on them all, most compassionate Jesus,
and draw them to your Sacred Heart.
You are the King, Lord,
not only of the faithful who have never forsaken you,

but also of those prodigal sons and daughters who
    have abandoned you;
grant that they may quickly return to your Father's house
so that they will not die alienated and unreconciled.
You are the King of those who are misguided
by erroneous opinions, or whom discord keeps far away.
Call them back to the holiness of your truth and
    unity of faith,
so that soon there may be one flock and one shepherd.
Lord, grant to your Church assurance of freedom
    and immunity from harm;
give peace and order to all nations,
and make the earth resound from pole to pole with
    one voice.
Praise be to the divine Heart that won our salvation;
to you be glory and honor forever.
Amen.

111. PRAYERS TO THE SACRED HEART
(1859 Directory)

I

Most Holy Heart of Jesus,
shower your blessings in abundant measure upon
    your holy church,
upon our pope, and upon all the clergy and religious;

to the just, grant perseverance; convert sinners;
enlighten unbelievers; bless relatives, friends, and
  benefactors;
assist the dying; deliver the souls in purgatory;
and extend over all hearts the healing compassion
  of your love.
Amen.

II

Most loving Jesus,
see how far your exceeding love has reached!
Of your own flesh and most precious blood,
you have prepared for me a divine table
in order to give yourself wholly to me.
What has impelled such extensions of your love?
Surely, nothing else but your most loving Heart.
Adorable Heart of Jesus, burning fire of divine charity,
receive my heart within your most sacred wound,
to the end that, in this school of love,
I may make a return of love to the God
who has given me such wondrous proofs of love.
Amen.

112. Invocations to the Sacred Heart

I
(Saint Margaret Mary Alacoque)

O Heart of love,
I put all my trust in you;
for I fear all things
from my own weakness,
but I hope for all things from your goodness.

II

Sacred Heart of Jesus,
I give myself to you through Mary.

III

Let us adore, thank, pray to, and console,
in the company of Mary Immaculate,
the most sacred and well-beloved Heart of Jesus
in the Eucharist!

IV

Blessed be the Most Sacred Heart of Jesus
in the Holy Eucharist!

113. LITANY OF THE SACRED HEART OF JESUS

Lord, have mercy	Lord, have mercy
Christ, have mercy	Christ, have mercy
Lord, have mercy	Lord, have mercy
God the Father in heaven	have mercy on us
God the Son, Redeemer of the world	have mercy on us
God the Holy Spirit	have mercy on us
Holy Trinity, one God	have mercy on us
Heart of Jesus, Son of the eternal Father	have mercy on us
Heart of Jesus, formed by the Holy Spirit in the womb of the Virgin Mother	have mercy on us
Heart of Jesus, one with the eternal Word	have mercy on us
Heart of Jesus, infinite in majesty	have mercy on us
Heart of Jesus, holy Temple of God	have mercy on us
Heart of Jesus, tabernacle of the Most High	have mercy on us
Heart of Jesus, house of God and gate of heaven	have mercy on us
Heart of Jesus, aflame with love for us	have mercy on us
Heart of Jesus, source of justice and love	have mercy on us

Heart of Jesus, full of goodness
and love

have mercy on us

Heart of Jesus, wellspring
of all virtue

have mercy on us

Heart of Jesus, worthy of all praise have mercy on us

Heart of Jesus, King and center
of all hearts

have mercy on us

Heart of Jesus, treasure house of
wisdom and knowledge

have mercy on us

Heart of Jesus, in whom there
dwells the fullness of God

have mercy on us

Heart of Jesus, in whom the Father
is well pleased

have mercy on us

Heart of Jesus, from whose fullness
we have all received

have mercy on us

Heart of Jesus, desire of
the eternal hills

have mercy on us

Heart of Jesus, patient and
full of mercy

have mercy on us

Heart of Jesus, generous to all
who turn to you

have mercy on us

Heart of Jesus, fountain of life
and holiness

have mercy on us

Heart of Jesus, atonement for
our sins

have mercy on us

Heart of Jesus, overwhelmed
with insults

have mercy on us

Heart of Jesus, broken for our sins have mercy on us

Heart of Jesus, obedient even to death	have mercy on us
Heart of Jesus, pierced by a lance	have mercy on us
Heart of Jesus, source of all consolation	have mercy on us
Heart of Jesus, our life and resurrection	have mercy on us
Heart of Jesus, our peace and reconciliation	have mercy on us
Heart of Jesus, victim of our sins	have mercy on us
Heart of Jesus, salvation of all who trust in you	have mercy on us
Heart of Jesus, hope of all who die in you	have mercy on us
Heart of Jesus, delight of all the saints	have mercy on us
Lamb of God, you take away the sins of the world	have mercy on us
Lamb of God, you take away the sins of the world	have mercy on us
Lamb of God, you take away the sins of the world	have mercy on us

Jesus, gentle and humble of heart,
—*Touch our hearts and make them like your own.*

Let us pray.

Father,
we rejoice in the gifts of love
we have received from the heart of Jesus your Son.
Open our hearts to share his life
and continue to bless us with his love.
We ask this in the name of Jesus the Lord.
Amen.

Or:

Grant, we pray, almighty God,
that we, who glory in the Heart of your beloved
    Son
and recall the wonders of his love for us,
may be made worthy to receive
an overflowing measure of grace
from that fount of heavenly gifts.
Through our Lord Jesus Christ, your Son,
who lives and reigns with you
in the unity of the Holy Spirit,
one God, forever and ever.
Amen.